Speak the Culture | Poland

Speak the Culture | Poland

PL

BE FLUENT IN POLISH LIFE AND CULTURE

HISTORY, SOCIETY AND LIFESTYLE • LITERATURE AND PHILOSOPHY

ART AND ARCHITECTURE • CINEMA AND FASHION

MUSIC AND DRAMA • FOOD AND DRINK • MEDIA AND SPORT

THOROGOOD

www.thorogoodpublishing.co.uk   www.speaktheculture.net

All has been done to trace the owners of the various pieces of material used for this book. If further information and proof of ownership should be made available then attribution will be given or, if requested, the said material removed in subsequent editions.

A CIP catalogue record for this book is available from the British Library.

ISBN: 1854187880
9781854187888

Thorogood Publishing Ltd
10-12 Rivington Street
London EC2A 3DU

Telephone: 020 7749 4748
Fax: 020 7729 6110
info@thorogoodpublishing.co.uk

www.thorogoodpublishing.co.uk
www.speaktheculture.net

© 2012
Thorogood Publishing Ltd

Old town in Warsaw

Publisher

Neil Thomas

Editorial Director
Angela Spall

Editor in chief

Andrew Whittaker

Additional editorial contributors
David Banks
Alexandra Fedoruk
Amy Wilson Thomas

Design & illustration

Phylip Harries
Richard Grosse
falconburydesign.co.uk

Johnny Bull
plumpState
plumpstate.com

Shutterstock

iStockphoto

Printed in the UK by
Ashford Colour Press

Acknowledgements

Special thanks to:
Joanna Agnieszka Harris
Cheryl Thomas
The Adam Mickiewicz
Institute, Warsaw,
in particular Aleksander
Laskowski, Agnieszka
Mrowińska and Paweł
Potoroczyn

Contents

First, a word from
the publisher...

This series of books and this book are designed to look at a country's culture – to give readers a real grasp of it and to help them develop and explore that culture.

The world is shrinking – made smaller by commerce, tourism and migration – and yet the importance of national culture, of national identity, seems to grow.

By increasing your cultural knowledge and appreciation of a country, be it your own or a foreign land, you reach a genuine understanding of the people and how they live.

We're talking about culture in all its guises: the creative arts that give a country its spirit as well as the culture of everyday life.

Speak the Culture books sit alongside guidebooks and language courses, serving not only as a companionable good read but also as an invaluable tool for understanding a country's current culture and its heritage.

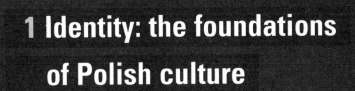

1 Identity: the foundations of Polish culture

1.1 Geography

Poland has always been in thrall to its landscape. Lying at the heart of Europe, with little in the way of natural boundaries, the territory has long been a crossroads for people and cultures.

1. Identity: the foundations of Polish culture

2. Literature and philosophy

3. Art, architecture and design

4. Music, theatre, and comedy

5. Cinema and fashion

6. Media and communications

7. Food and drink

8. Living culture, the state of modern Poland

Naming Polska

Poles generally refer to their own country as 'Polska', although the official term is Rzeczpospolita Polska (Republic of Poland). The name is derivative of 'Polans', the Western Slavic tribe that came to dominate the Polish lowlands in the tenth century. Over the centuries, Polish writers have sometimes referred to their country as Lechia, after Lech (brother of Czech and Rus), a legendary Slav often credited with establishing the Polish nation.

Stuck in the middle

Poland lies in the centre of Europe, as close to the Atlantic Ocean as it is to the Ural Mountains. The culture here has been shaped by this location, influenced by the ebb and flow of Slavic, Germanic, Baltic and Jewish elements over the centuries to emerge as something distinctly 'Polish'. Today, the country's north-western border is open to the Baltic Sea; the rest of Poland is locked in by other nations, namely (clockwise from the Baltic) Russia (in the enclave oblast of Kaliningrad), Lithuania, Belarus, Ukraine, Slovakia, Czech Republic and Germany.

Lie of the land

The dominant physical feature of the Polish landscape is an extensive central plain – a lowland sweep of forest and field that has always left the country vulnerable to invasion and foreign rule, but which, equally, has encouraged the easy assimilation of cultures and peoples. On the southern frontiers, the lowlands give way first to hills and then to the Sudeten and Carpathian Mountains. The highest peaks are in the Carpathians, in particular the Tatra Mountains that line the border with Slovakia.

Poland's largest rivers, the Oder (in the west) and the Vistula (central), drain into the Baltic Sea at either end of the country's 300-mile long coastline, along which spits, lagoons, dunes and saltmarshes predominate. The country is also blessed with thousands of lakes (in Europe, only Finland has more in such density), the largest collection being in the Mazurian Lake District in the north-east. In the borderlands with Belarus, the Białowieża forest (one of 23 Polish national parks) is a last surviving fragment of the primeval woodland that once covered Europe's lowlands.

What's the weather like?

The Polish climate is often described as 'moderate' – a label to cling to when you're shivering through the depths of a foggy, freezing winter in the central plains. Indeed, the country's 'central' location, open to both maritime and continental airflows, generates a fickle climate that can vary significantly from year to year. However, a few generalisations can be applied: the maritime airflows of northern and western Poland bring relatively soft, humid winters and wet cool summers; whilst the continental air of the south and east can deliver bitter winters and hot summers, both of them relatively dry. The Poles sometimes talk about six seasons, squeezing an early spring (*przedwiośnie*) and early autumn (*przedzimie*) into the traditional calendar. And autumn isn't just autumn, it's the Golden Polish Autumn (*Złota Polska Jesień*). Culturally, the weather is a default conversation opener in Poland as it is elsewhere. In the years of Soviet rule, when the weather forecast was often more reliable than the news, TV forecasters became very popular, in particular Czesław Nowicki, nicknamed *Wicherek* (Breeze), and his female equivalent, Elżbieta Sommer, or *Chmurka* (Small Cloud).

An evil wind…

Poland has a fabled wind, the *wiatr halny*. It's a foehn wind, usually a southerly created when air hits the mountains, rises rapidly, warms and then blows intensely down the mountains' leeward slopes. Trees are felled, tiles ripped off roofs and, if the wind strikes in winter, snows rapidly thawed leading to floods and avalanches. Some think it also induces a mental malaise in the local population. The Góral highlanders of Podhale in the Tatra Mountains have woven the *wiatr halny* into their culture, using it in stories and poems.

Area: 120,727 sq miles (312,685 sq km) (similar in size to Italy, or New Mexico)

Highest mountain: Mount Rysy 8,200 ft (2,499m)

Longest river: Vistula 651 miles (1,047km)

Population: 38 million

Life expectancy: 72 for men, 80 for women

Median age: 38

Wanda takes one for the team

There are several legends about Princess Wanda, daughter of Krakus, mythical founder of Kraków. One has her committing suicide by jumping into the Vistula. Having repelled the amorous advances and armies of a German prince, Wanda leapt into the river to save Poland from a possible procession of invasive suitors disgruntled at the princess' refusal to lie back and (not) think of Poland.

Where do the Poles live?

In the second half of the 20th century, Poland matured from a largely rural society into one in which the majority of the population (almost two thirds) became urban. The major change occurred in the 30 years after the Second World War, hastened by the country's rapid industrialisation and reconstruction. However, the scale of urbanisation has been less pronounced in Poland than in other developed nations, and Polish towns and cities remain relatively small and scattered. Only Warsaw has a population exceeding one million. Equally, Poland's post-war experience may have created a wider cultural gulf between town and country than elsewhere in Europe. Poland's peasant farming tradition survived remarkably well, even dodging Soviet collectivisation (unlike other Eastern Bloc countries), and rural areas have subsequently lagged – socially, materially and culturally – behind the towns and cities where rapid modernisation brought change to all spheres of life. Today, it seems the tide of movement from country to town has peaked.

Poland was rearranged into 16 provinces, or *województwo*, in 1999. Some correspond to historic regions (or portions thereof) dating back as far as the Middle Ages. Others have been hacked from more recent maps with expediency rather than history in mind. Even so, most have a distinct landscape and culture. All have an elected assembly *(sejmik)* and a governor (*wojewoda*).

North-west

Zachodniopomorskie (West Pomerania)
With long dune-backed Baltic beaches, lakes, the odd bison and a sparse population, Poland's north-western corner is one of its least spoilt. For centuries, West Pomerania had Prussian rulers, and much of the region has only been Polish since 1945, when the German population was resettled westwards. Surviving medieval mercantile buildings recall the region's Hanseatic League

connections, although most towns were devastated by the Second World War. The island of Wolin has older roots; Pagan Slavs ('Pomeranians') traded with Vikings from here in the eighth century.

Pomorskie (Pomerania)
The eastern chunk of old Pomerania was returned to Poland in 1919 after centuries of Prussian rule. The region abounds in lakes, set in rolling countryside; on the coast, the dunes of the Hel Peninsula and resorts like Sopot draw summer tourists. Gdańsk, rebuilt to its Hanseatic blueprint after the Second World War, links with Sopot and Gdynia to form a large conurbation. In the central lake-land region of Kashubia, the people retain the traditions and languages of their Western Slavic ancestors.

The lands that make up modern-day Poland have been arranged in many different ways over the centuries. Some of the old boundaries and identities live on in the collective consciousness, recalled today when referring to certain parts of the country:

Pomerania. The region along the southern shore of the Baltic Sea, covering what is now north-eastern Germany and north-western Poland as far as the Vistula; controlled variously by Poland, the Holy Roman Empire, Prussia, Germany and Sweden.

Galicia. Curling around the north-western flank of the Carpathian Mountains into western Ukraine and up into southern Poland; part of the Austrian Empire up to the First World War.

Silesia. The basin of the upper Oder Valley, mostly contained in modern-day Poland, but with small enclaves in Germany and the Czech Republic; Polish in the Middle Ages, then Bohemian, Austrian (Habsburg), Prussian and German before becoming Polish again in 1945.

Lubuskie (Lubusz)

You have to go back a long way (to the tenth century world of Mieszko I) to find the Polish roots of Lubusz; origins rekindled in 1945 when the region was finally wrested back from centuries of Prussian rule (a new Polish population was resettled from the east). Lubusz is chiefly rural – the landscape relatively flat and peppered with swamps, lakes and forests. Two small cities, Gorzów Wielkopolski (north) and Zielona Góra (south) are known, respectively, for oil extraction and wine.

North-east

Warmińsko-Mazuskie (Warmia-Masuria)

As the name suggests, Warmia-Masuria comprises two historic provinces. Both (Warmia to the west and Masuria to the east) were ceded back to Poland in 1945 after centuries under the yoke of East Prussia. Today, the region's Polish population lives alongside a large number of ethnic Ukrainians, relocated here by the same post-war Communist regime that ordered German residents to leave. The further west you venture, the more primordial the scenery feels; it's a mix of dark forests, deserted swamps and pristine post-glacial lakes (including the Great Mazurian Lakes). Gothic castles – left behind by the Teutonic Knights – add to the Middle-earth ambiance.

Podlaskie

Podlaskie, marshy in the north and forested to the south, is the most sparsely populated region in Poland. Bordering Belarus and Lithuania (and inclusive of minority Belarusian and Lithuanian populations), at times it feels like a land untouched, a place where vast ancient woodlands and swamps conceal lynx, elk, bison and wolves. Historically, creeds and cultures have mixed well in Podlaskie, with Muslims (Tartars), Jews (now gone), Orthodox (Belarusian) and Catholics managing to co-exist. The main city, Białystok, an industrial affair, lies north-west of Białowieża Forest, Poland's most prized national park.

Central

Wielkopolska (Greater Poland)

Many regard 'Greater Poland' as the cradle of the Polish state. Here, under the Piast dynasty in the tenth century, the Polonie built their first royal domain. In the centuries that followed, the area remained more 'Polish' than its Germanised neighbours. Like much of Poland to the north, parts of the region abound in glaciated lakes; the rest is a mix of rolling farmland and forest. More of the country's historic buildings have survived here than elsewhere, not least Gniezno's Gothic cathedral and Rogalin's neoclassical Raczyński Palace. The big city is Poznań, although Gniezno was Poland's first capital.

Kujawsko-Pomorskie

The central-northern area of Kujawsko-Pomorskie brings its two historical constituents – split by the Vistula –

together under a modern-day administration. Physically, the region is characterised by the agricultural lowlands bordering its many rivers. Architecturally, Toruń, a Hanseatic city of redbrick Gothic buildings that merits its place on UNESCO's World Heritage List, is popular, although numerous smaller towns, such as Chełmno, have their medieval churches and castles built by the Teutonic Knights. Bydgoszcz is a more workaday city.

Mittel Europe

In 1775 the small town of Suchowola in Podlaski was crowned the geographic centre of Europe, as deduced by royal astronomer Szymon Antoni Sobiekrajski. A brass plaque still marks the spot.

Smaller but greater

Wielkopolska (Greater Poland) and Małopolska (Lesser Poland), along with parts of Silesia, formed the heartland of the medieval Polish state. Those prefixes (Greater and Lesser) don't refer to size, but rather to running order in the nation-building process – 'greater' really meaning 'older'. Indeed, the original Małopolska territory (much larger than the current administrative district of the same name) was bigger in size than Wielkopolska, and had Kraków, the old capital, at its heart.

Łódzkie

Named for its largest city, an industrial titan built on a 19th century textile boom, the Łódzkie region is in the middle of Poland and therefore Europe; a location borne out by its post-modern growth as a hub for business, education and culture. The city, already famous for its film school (see section 5.1.2), has filled its defunct industrial buildings with museums, exhibitions and festivals in the years since 1989. Much of the region's landscape has been shaped by the rivers that have helped create fertile farmland around the pockets of industry. In the southern half of the region, the terrain starts to rise with the beginnings of Poland's uplands.

Mazowieckie (Masovia)

Poland's largest, wealthiest and most populous region is a historic territory with Warsaw at its heart. In Masovia, Poland's post-Communist development is at its most vigorous; the dourness of the Soviet era replaced by foreign investment, café culture and bold

new architecture. Warsaw is the main beneficiary, its attentively rebuilt Old (13th and 14th centuries) and New (16th century) Towns and the modern city centre increasingly surrounded by shiny new buildings amongst the drab tower blocks. The countryside around Warsaw and the region's other large urban areas – Radom, Płock and Siedlce – is rolling arable farmland and woodland, including the ancient Kampinoska Forest that meets the edge of Warsaw. Large mansions and partially demolished castles, redolent of the region's prosperous history, dot the countryside.

	Population in 1939	Population in 1945
Białystok	107,000	56,000
Warsaw	1.3 million	422,000

South

Dolnoslaskie (Lower Silesia)

Historically, Lower Silesia has been German or Bohemian more often than Polish, only really joining the fold in 1945. The remnants of this multicultural past are found in the buildings (from medieval castles to Baroque palaces), not in the people – much of the region's current population was installed from Polish Ukraine (specifically Lwów) after the war. The big city is Wrocław, carefully reconstructed from wartime ruins and well chosen for its role as European Capital of Culture in 2016. Scenically, southern Lower Silesia draws the crowds with the Karkonosze section of the Sudety Mountains, and also boasts the largest timber-framed churches (the Churches of Peace) in the world.

Opolskie (Opole)

The modest province of Opole, with a small, formerly Piast city of the same name at its centre, has historically been included within Silesia. Unlike Lower Silesia to the north, however, Opole has retained a German minority (about ten per cent of the population), and the influence of Germanic culture has endured here more than elsewhere in Poland. The region's north is forested, the south farmed until the Opawskie Mountains rise up to the

Opole on song

The city of Opole stages Poland's glitziest music festival, the National Festival of Polish Song (Krajowy Festiwal Piosenki Polskiej). An event to rival Italy's annual San Remo sing-off, the festival has been held every year since 1963, apart from in 1982 when martial law got in the way.

Czech Republic border. Quarries dot the landscape; and the rock here periodically throws up fossilised dinosaurs.

Śląskie (Silesia)

Hewn from the old identity of 'Upper Silesia', Silesia is another Polish region with strong historical links to Germany. An early 20th century plebiscite split the region between ethnic Poles and Germans, although most of the latter were expelled after the Second World War. Nevertheless, the region retains a mixed 'Silesian' culture of Polish, Germanic and other influences. For decades, Silesia has been famous for its heavy industry (and pollution) – coal mining and steel production in particular – and with the city of Katowice as a hub, the region contains Poland's biggest urban sprawl. Nevertheless, the landscape, particularly the Beskidy Mountains in the south, can be spectacular.

Małopolska (Lesser Poland)

Lesser Poland is the most visited province in the country. The main draw is Kraków, former seat of the Piast dynasty, and the only large Polish city that wasn't flattened in the Second World War. The huge market square (Rynek Główny) in the old town, and Wawel Hill, the spiritual heart of Poland, with its cathedral and former royal castle overlooking the Vistula, are two of numerous attractions. Nearby, Auschwitz Birkenau German Nazi Concentration and Extermination Camp recalls the grim fate of Jews from Kraków and elsewhere. Małopolska is hilly or mountainous, particularly in the Podhale region to the south (here lie the Tatras), where

the wooden town of Zakopane, a hub for Góral culture, inspired a folksy and patriotic creative awakening in the early 20th century (see section 3.2.3).

Świętokrzyskie

Taking its name from the ancient, crumbling 'Holy Cross' mountain range (a focus for partisan resistance in the Second World War), Świętokrzyskie is a small, often overlooked region. Those that do come here regularly do so to take the waters; others visit for the caves, monasteries and ruined castles, or to ski and hike in the undulating, forested hills. The main city is Kielce, one-time outpost of Tsarist Russia, whilst the villages that pepper the region can be quiet, dilapidated and charming.

Podkarpackie

Sharing its borders with Slovakia and Ukraine, in Poland's south-eastern corner, much of Podkarpackie is returning to wilderness. Two Carpathian mountain ranges, the Bieszczady and the Beskid Niski, are almost empty of people, many of their old inhabitants – Ukrainians and the Boyko and Lemko ethnic groups – having been forcibly removed after the war. Winsome Orthodox churches hidden in the forests recall the region's former occupants, as do the folkloric traditions still acted out in villages packed with wooden architecture. Rzeszów is the capital; Łańcut Castle the opulent aristocratic pile nearby.

Lubelskie (Lublin)

In common with the other borderlands in the east, Lubelskie's tradition of cultural tolerance was swept aside in the mid 20th century and only survives in the remnant mix of Catholic, Orthodox and Jewish temples. Nowhere is this more keenly felt than in Lublin city, once called the Polish Jerusalem. Today, the city is a mix of charming old buildings and new enterprise (the student population is large). The Lubelskie landscape is largely flat, its fields perfect for grain production; grand churches and mansions were once built on the profits. Small churches, tatty wooden houses and the immovable concrete remains of the Mołotow Line can be found in the dense tracts of forest.

Small town humour

The small Świętokrzyskie town of Wąchock is known throughout Poland as the butt of various jokes. Many feature the town's *sołtys*, the generic 'small town' mayor; others simply poke fun at the general level of intellect. For example: Q: Why did the residents of Wąchock build a higher bell tower? A: Because the bell rope was too long.

Wooden idols

Podkarpackie has a bountiful section of the national 'Wooden Architecture Trail'. The route through the region features 127 buildings in all, including the 15th century church at Haczów, the oldest wooden church in Poland and, apparently, the biggest such Gothic building in the world.

1.2 History

Much of Poland's recent history –
with its anguished tales of partition
and invasion – makes for grim
reading. However, explore the long
view and the portrait of a strong,
progressive nation begins to emerge.

1.2.1 Enlightened beginnings: the Piasts and medieval Poland

Key dates

5000BC The first Neolithic farmers drift up from the Danube.

600AD The Polanie tribe dominate the Warta basin.

966 Piast Duke Mieszko I adopts Catholicism.

1025 Bolesław the Brave crowned first Polish king.

1226 The Teutonic Knights conquer northern Poland.

1365 University of Kraków founded.

1386 Poland marries into the Lithuanian Jagiellonian dynasty.

1410 Poland and Lithuania defeat the Teutonic Knights in the Battle of Grunwald.

1569 Commonwealth of the Two Nations formally unites Poland and Lithuania.

Plain speaking

The Polanie were known as 'the people of the fields' (i.e. they lived on the plain).

Polish by design; Catholic by necessity

The Romans didn't make it to Poland. Impenetrable Carpathian forests and Germanic longhairs put them off. Instead, the large lowland plains of central northern Europe were colonised by Celts and then Western Slavs. One tribe in particular, the Polanie, were established in the Warta basin by the seventh century. The pagan Polanie developed a powerful ruling dynasty, the Piast princes of Gniezno. With an army, castles and a system of taxation, the Piasts strengthened their fledgling territory, Wielkopolska, over the next 200 years. Under Mieszko I they drew in other tribes – close cultural kin with a similar language – and by 990, in alliance with other Slavs in Małopolska and Silesia, the ruler had established a nascent Polish nation state. It was a Roman Catholic affair; Mieszko had assuaged the threat of invasion from Holy Roman Emperor, Otto III, land grabbing to the west, by converting his territories to Christianity in 966.

Life with the Piasts

Mieszko I's son, Bolesław the Brave, was the first crowned king of Poland. Emperor Otto III effectively bestowed the title on Bolesław during the Congress of Gniezno in 1000, although Bolesław made certain with another coronation 25 years later, by which time he'd consumed bits of Bohemia, Ukraine and Pomerania into the country that was now officially recognised as Poland (and which looked remarkably similar in shape to its modern-day incarnation). The Piast kings that followed over the next 350 years did their best to preserve Bolesław's kingdom.

The capital moved to Kraków in the mid 11th century, where Bolesław II scored a dramatic own goal with the assassination of the city's bishop; the all-powerful clergy duly deposed the king. Bolesław III (the Wrymouth) rebuilt power but undid the good work by splitting Poland amongst four of his sons. Feudalised, the country

18

The Iron Age fort at Biskupin

lumbered through the 12th century. In Mazovia, a northern duke opened Pandora's box when he asked crusading Teutonic Knights to help him control pagan Prussians along the Baltic coast in the 1220s; the Prussians were expelled but the Knights seized much of Wielkopolska, built almighty castles and cut Poland off from the sea. Brutal incursions by Tartars from the east also weakened 13th century Poland, if only temporarily. Nevertheless, the Piasts remained in power throughout and the young Polish state survived and rebuilt. The accession of Władysław the Elbow-high ('vertically challenged' in today's parlance) in 1306 finally brought the Polish lands back under centralised control – and the country positively flourished under his son, Kazimierz III (the Great).

Marrying into the Jagiellonians

By the end of Kazimierz III's progressive reign, Poland had ceded any claim to Silesia but had secured its southern borders with Bohemia, made peace with the Teutonic Knights and won new territory to the east. In Kraków the king created a multicultural city of learning,

Digging up the past

The area that became Poland has been inhabited for 800,000 years, since the early Stone Age, but the best prehistoric footprint was left by the Iron Age Lusatian culture. A fortified Lusatian fort from circa 700BC was unearthed at Biskupin in Weilkospolska in 1933 and held up as a symbol of early Slavic (and therefore Polish) resistance to neighbouring Germanic tribes. When Poland was occupied in 1939, the Nazis continued excavating (under the patronage of Heinrich Himmler), renamed the site Urstadt and wrote the story of how Iron Age Germanic tribes had overrun the Lusatian fort. The original interpretation and name were reinstated when the Nazis left.

The new Prussians

The Teutonic Knights, aka The Order of the House of St Mary of the Germans in Jerusalem, were Christian guns for hire (in the days before guns). Duke Konrad of Mazovia contracted them out in 1226, offering land in exchange for converting the truculent Prussians. In the event, the Knights slaughtered the Prussians and took up residence in northern Poland (including Gdańsk, which they renamed Danzig). The order was a thorn in Poland's side for the next 300 years, but it did deposit northern Poland's finest medieval architecture: a collection of large red brick fortresses. Such was the length of their tenure that the Knights themselves – efficient, expansionist and commercially advanced – eventually became known as the Prussians. Their Order is still going today.

Malbork Castle

1. Identity: the foundations of Polish culture 2. Literature and philosophy 3. Art, architecture and design 4. Music, theatre and comedy 5. Cinema and fashion 6. Media and communications 7. Food and drink 8. Living culture: the state of modern Poland

Poland was one of most tolerant, multicultural states in medieval Europe. It was a Christian country yet welcomed (and gave refuge to) Jews fleeing pogroms in Western Europe in the 11th and 12th centuries. In 1334 Kazimierz the Great gave Jews freedom of movement and trade, and legal protection, and on the fringe of Kraków founded Kazimierz, which remained a centre for Jewish learning, trade and culture right through to 1939. Similarly, when Kazimierz took territory in Red Ruthenia and Podolia (both present-day Ukraine), the conquered Armenian and Eastern Orthodox minorities retained their faith.

'HE FOUND POLAND BUILT OF WOOD, AND LEFT HER IN STONE.'
Famous Polish saying about Kazimierz the Great

commerce and grand architecture. When he died with no male heir, the Piast dynasty came to an end, but the Polish monarchy found renewed vigour with the marriage of Queen Jadwiga to Grand Duke Władysław II Jagiełło of Lithuania in 1386. The union created a prosperous political alliance with the Grand Duchy of Lithuania (a newly (and only partially) Christianised state that covered as much territory as Poland, directly

on its eastern flank) that would last for 400 years. It also placed Poland under the sovereignty of the Jagiellonian dynasty.

On honeymoon with Lithuania

Under Jagiełło, who outlived his queen by 45 years, Poland and Lithuania became the strongest political entity in central Europe. The allied states took the fight to the Teutonic Knights, beginning with victory at the Battle of Grunwald in 1410 and following up with the Thirteen Years War (1454-66) that freed Gdańsk (as an independent city state paying homage to the Jagiellonians) and brought Prussia under Polish control. It was a golden age for the region, particularly its nobility, which retained significant autonomy under the king (they formed the *sejm*, an early parliament). As the Italian Renaissance filtered north in the 16th century, encouraged by Kraków's hotline to Rome, so learning and the arts flourished. The region also remained a rare bastion of religious tolerance (extended even to Lutherans). Needless to say, however, it wasn't all good times and backslaps: ongoing incursions by the Muscovite Tsars, Ottomans and Crimean Tartars shortened the Jagiellonians' reach in the south and east. The Russian threat convinced the last of the Jagiellonian kings to formalise Poland's relationship with Lithuania, and the Commonwealth of the Two Nations was born at the Union of Lublin in 1569.

Democracy for the nobs

The Commonwealth, or Rzeczpospolita, that bound Poland and the Grand Duchy of Lithuania together (with much of modern-day Ukraine and Belarus included) in 1569 was progressive for its time. With a constitution devised by Renaissance scholars, the state was a democracy of sorts; one that elected kings in an era when royals still ruled by divine right. Admittedly, only landowners (the *szlachta* drawn from all areas of the Commonwealth and equating to less than ten per cent of the population) could vote but, nevertheless, they established local assemblies to elect ministers to the parliament – now relocated to Warsaw, the capital from 1596 – which then voted on new legislation.

The Republic of Nobles, as the state was known, looked impressively egalitarian alongside the absolutist monarchies developing elsewhere in Europe. There was a failing though: it strengthened the region's feudal tradition, shoring up the power of local landholders who would later be open to suggestion from invading foreign powers. Culturally, the Commonwealth maintained the region's mix of languages, ethnicities and religions – the 1573 Compact of Warsaw even confirmed the freedom of religion in writing.

Holding back the tide, just

Over two centuries, a procession of monarchs (both Polish and foreign) was elected to rule the Rzeczpospolita. Most, such as Stefan Batory, Duke of Transylvania, who beat back the Russians in 1582, were measured by their success at waging war (often dependent on their ability to raise a war chest from the powerful nobles). Under the Waza dynasty, which gave Poland three consecutive kings in the first half of the 17th century, the power of the Commonwealth slowly eroded, ceded in particular to Prussia and Sweden, the latter imperious after victory in the Thirty Years War (in which the Rzeczpospolita remained neutral).

Key dates

1573 The Compact of Warsaw formalises a long-held religious tolerance.

1648 Two decades of devastation begin, including the Swedish Deluge.

1683 Victory in the Battle of Vienna hastens the Ottoman Empire's demise.

1764 The last elected king, Stanisław II August Poniatowski, takes to the throne.

1795 Third Partition destroys the Rzeczpospolita, and the independent Polish state disappears.

1815 The Congress Kingdom of Poland (around Warsaw) and Free City of Kraków are created, under tight Russian control.

1846 The unsuccessful Kraków Uprising sees the city annexed by Austria.

Chin up, someday this will make a great film

The Deluge, in which Charles X of Sweden overran much of Poland (Russia overran the remainder), began in 1648 and unfurled in a series of campaigns that lasted nearly 20 years. Having gained control along the Baltic coast, Charles put the rest of Poland to the sword, burning crops and destroying towns and villages. Famine followed, exacerbated by plague. Opinions vary on how many actually died, but conservative estimates suggest at least a quarter of the population perished in the decade after 1650. Positivist author Henryk Sienkiewicz (see section 2.1.4) set a favourite Polish novel, *Potop* (1886), in the Deluge; it was the second book in a trilogy about the Rzeczpospolita. Jerzy Hoffman directed a popular film adaptation of Sienkiewicz's book in 1974.

Under the third Waza, Jan Kazimierz, wars against the Russians in the east and the Swedes to the north decimated the Polish people. The Swedes' incursion and subsequent occupation became known as the Deluge (*Potop*). Up to half of the population died. However, the Commonwealth fought back – its armies were often outnumbered but famously slick – and regained much of its territory, if not its dominance in central Europe – that was gone; Russia was now the main player. Internally, the parliament became increasingly unworkable, sabotaged by a constitutional flaw that enabled any member to veto legislation.

Neighbours from hell

In the later 17th century, the increasingly decrepit Rzeczpospolita triumphed in the battles of Khotyn (1673) and Vienna (1683), where commander Jan Sobieski halted the advance of the Ottoman Empire, but the victories came at the cost of security elsewhere – Prussia and Austria strengthened whilst Poland dealt with the Turks. Sobieski was elected king for his efforts. A Saxon king, Augustus II the Strong, elected for his money, replaced Sobieski but was a weak ruler who made Poland a battleground once more, pulled in different directions by Prussia, Russia, Sweden and Saxony. When Augustus was deposed and replaced with a Pole, Stanisław Leszczyński, the neighbours moved in and fought each other on Polish soil. Russia won out and took effective control, ostensibly as 'protector' of the Rzeczpospolita but in reality as puppeteer. The Commonwealth limped on for another 50 years, trying but failing to rebuild the economy and to reassert its independence. Whilst Russia controlled eastern Poland, Prussia seized Silesia in the west. Finally, in 1772, Prussia, Austria and Russia chose to partition Poland rather than continue fighting over it.

Poland partitioned

There were three 'Partitions' of Poland in the later 18th century, each more invasive than the last. The First Partition ceded almost a third of Polish territory, given to Austria, Russia and Prussia on the respective flanks, yet the country remained relatively stable. King Stanisław II August Poniatowski stayed on the throne and the Poles, under his guidance, retained their progressive politics, reforming the constitution to give the bourgeoisie a share in power and improving the lot of the peasantry. Wary of such liberalism (and the boost it might give to Polish identity), Catherine the Great, Empress of Russia, invaded. The Poles put up a fight, inspired by

Stanisław August
Poniatowski
(1732 – 1798)

Lingering golden
age glow

The word Rzeczpospolita is regularly used as a catch-all term for the Polish state (the Republic), but it also has a specific application to the Polish-Lithuanian Commonwealth of the 16th to 18th centuries (indeed, Rzeczpospolita is often translated as 'Commonwealth' (and equally, as 'Republic')). Contemporaneous descriptions of the Rzeczpospolita included Res Publica Serenissima, the Most Serene Republic, and this concept of a 'golden age' lives on in the Polish psyche. The Rzeczpospolita is held up as a beacon of tolerance, a multi-national state that accepted different creeds and ethnicities, promoted learning, and which enfranchised a significant proportion of the population.

1. Identity: the
foundations
of Polish culture

2. Literature
and philosophy

3. Art, architecture
and design

4. Music, theatre,
and comedy

5. Cinema
and fashion

6. Media and
communications

7. Food and drink

8. Living culture:
the state of
modern Poland

Have I shown you my porcelain collection?

What Augustus II the Strong lacked in military prowess he compensated for with brawn. The sobriquet referred to an impressive physical strength, allegedly capable of snapping horseshoes in two. His physical prowess extended to the bedroom – Augustus fathered more than 300 children, although only one, Augustus III, was legitimate. The king is also remembered for his patronage of the arts, in particular his success at manufacturing fine porcelain for the first time outside China (or at least in commissioning Johann Friedrich Böttger to do so).

Culture in exile

The repressive climate of the 19th century – particularly in the Russian-held part of Poland – convinced many of Poland's finest creative figures to live in exile. A number settled in Paris, including the composer Fryderyk Chopin, and poets Adam Mickiewicz and Cyprian Norwid, from where they fanned the fires of rebellion back home.

Tadeusz Kościuszko, veteran of the American War of Independence, but lost and Catherine imposed the Second Partition in 1793, tearing up the constitution and allocating more territory to Russia and Prussia (including prized Danzig). In what remained of their nation, the Poles made one last stand, again led by General Kościuszko: they rose up against the Russians in 1794, but, despite a celebrated victory at the Battle of Racławice, lost the war. The Russians removed the king from power and installed the Third Partition in 1795, dividing the remaining Polish territories between Russia, Austria and Prussia.

Poland in mind, if not body

Poland had been wiped from the map of Europe, but survived as a cultural entity. Indeed, even though it wouldn't reappear as a political being for another 123 years, and even whilst many Poles emigrated (to North America in particular), throughout Poland's subjugation national identity remained strong, carried along by language, tradition, militiamen and the growing nationalism of its Catholic faith.

Various attempts were made to fight off the occupying powers. Józef Poniatowski, nephew of the last king, joined forces with Napoleon but was heroically defeated in 1812. The Duchy of Warsaw and the free city of Kraków came and went, but helped to keep Polish identity alive. In the Russian sector, the armed uprisings of 1830 and 1863 intensified the authorities' efforts to suppress Polish culture, whilst in Silesia and East Prussia, the *Kulturkamp* of the industrialising German rulers similarly tried to stifle the local beliefs and language (Polish was outlawed). Usually, such measures only strengthened the Poles' resolve to preserve their identity.

Opening the door to independence

The Poles entered the 20th century still without a nation state. However, Russian and German (and to a much lesser extent, Austrian) attempts to crush Polish culture had failed. The territory's natural resources and industrious spirit had created centres of growth (if not wealth for the Poles) in places like Łódź (textiles) and Silesia (coal). Here, the urban working classes could be organised and mobilised. A wave of strikes called for reform in 1905– one of the loudest voices was novelist Henryk Sienkiewicz – before, a year later, Józef Piłsudski, an inveterate malcontent, established secret militia, training men to fight for independence. When the First World War broke out in 1914, Piłsudski organised his militarised groups into the Polish Legions, numbering some 14,000 men.

Rising from the ashes

The imperialist Partition powers fought each other in the First World War (Germany and Austria lined up against Russia) and Poland became a battleground. The Poles were conscripted to either side, with Piłsudski and his Polish Legions initially taking up arms for Austria against the Russians, before turning their sights on Germany when Russia dissolved into revolution. The Eastern Front ranged across Poland, devastating the land and killing more than a million Poles, until at the war's end, with the occupying

Curie supports the cause

In 1903 Marie Skłodowska-Curie won the first of two Nobel prizes for work in radiation (the second came in 1911). Marie had grown up in partitioned Poland, in a family that had been stripped of its possessions after involvement in nationalist uprisings. She studied at Warsaw's 'Flying University', a clandestine institution that resisted the Russification of Polish education, before moving to Paris where she remained for much her subsequent life (taking French citizenship). Marie returned to Poland sporadically and ensured that her daughters learned the Polish language. During the First World War she actively championed the cause of an independent Poland, and in 1932 founded the Radium Institute in Warsaw. Curie also named polonium, the first chemical element she discovered, after her homeland.

Key Dates

1914 Józef Piłsudski commands the Polish Legions on the outbreak of the First World War.

1918 Independence is regained with Piłsudski as head of state.

1920 The 'Miracle on the Vistula' speeds victory in the Polish-Soviet war.

1926 Piłsudski seizes power in a coup d'état.

1939 Nazi Germany invades Poland; Russia does the same within weeks.

1944 As the Warsaw Uprising fails, the Germans raze the city to the ground.

1947 Rigged elections install the Polish Communists in power.

1980 The Gdańsk Agreement legalises the Solidarność trade union movement.

1981 General Jaruzelski declares martial law.

1989 Round Table talks lead to democratic elections and the end of Communist rule.

1999 Poland joins NATO.

2004 Poland joins the European Union.

The Young Poland (Młoda Polska) movement emerged at the turn of the 20th century. Writers, composers, architects, artists and playwrights eschewed the rationale of Positivism (the dominant cultural trend in late 19th century Poland) in favour of a dreamy, decadent, neo-Romanticism that hoped to stir Poland from its century of servitude. Młoda Polska had similarities with Art Nouveau, but was more combative, blending native folk traditions with mysticism to reinvigorate Polish identity. The protagonists met in Kraków's cafés; the city fell within the Austrian Empire, and was thus more tolerant of new ideas than elsewhere in partitioned Poland. Often, they decamped to Zakopane, the village in Podhale where Polish folk traditions remained strong. Stanisław Wyspiański – painter, playwright and designer – was the leading light.

powers defeated or exhausted, Poland finally regained independence. Piłsudski was given command of the fledgling Regency Council in November 1918, and soon became the recognised head of state.

A brief taste of freedom

Poland, newly independent, took four years to establish its borders after the First World War. The Paris Conference gave access to the Baltic Sea through the 'Polish Corridor', which isolated East Prussia from the rest of Germany and made Danzig a free city. However, the big showdown came with the newly assembled Soviet Union. The Red Army invaded Poland in 1920 and reached the gates of Warsaw before Piłsudski's forces fought back – the 'Miracle on the Vistula' turned the tide and helped push the eastern Polish border into old Lithuania. Soon after, Upper Silesia was split in two, and half given to Poland (the remainder stayed in Germany). The Poland that emerged was still multicultural (a third of its population made up of minorities), although it wasn't the harmonious melting pot of old – conflicts with Lithuania and Ukraine had created bad blood, and a wave of anti-Semitism added to the tension.

The democratic Second Polish Republic was always going to struggle. Piłsudski resigned in 1922, frustrated at the lack of cohesion, and was followed by four years of instability (which included the assassination of his successor). He returned to government via military coup in 1926 and went on to rule as de facto dictator until his death nine years later. Industry slowly wound into life and independence generated a flourish in the arts, but rural Poland remained woefully unmodernised. As the country's internal malaise continued, it failed to arm itself adequately against the threat that now emerged from Hitler's Germany. Having signed a pact with the Soviet Union to partition Poland in the event of war, on 1st September 1939, Hitler invaded. Two and a half weeks later, the Soviets attacked from the east. The brief, lame Second Republic was over.

The Warsaw Uprising

Ruined but resilient in the Second World War

Initially, the Second World War split Poland between Germany and the USSR, until the Nazis pushed the Soviets out in 1941 (but not before Stalin had sent over a million Poles to the gulags). A Polish government in exile was established in Paris and then London. Hitler saw the Slavic Poles as an inferior race and their land as *lebensraum* (living space) for the Aryans. The Nazis established concentration and extermination camps across Poland. They killed three million Jews and a million Poles; millions of others were taken to Germany and used for slave labour. A heroic Home Army emerged to resist, and did so famously in the Warsaw Uprising of 1944 that only fell on the Soviets' failure to help the rebels take the city from the Nazis – Stalin already had plans to annex Poland at the war's end and wasn't going to assist the rebellion. An earlier revolt, the Warsaw Ghetto

The fate of Poland's Jews

Within months of invading in 1939, the Nazis began confining Poland's Jews to ghettos. In larger cities, the ghettos were placed in the poorest areas and walled-in like prisons. Food was bought from the Germans with whatever means the Jews had left; hunger was widespread, as was disease and arbitrary violence, leading to thousands of deaths. Often, there was no electricity or sewerage. The Warsaw ghetto was the largest in the Third Reich, with more than 400,000 occupants living in an area of 1.3 miles square, several families to an apartment. In 1942 the Germans began liquidating the ghettos, transporting Jews to extermination camps by cattle truck. By 1944, with all ghettos liquidated, fewer than 100,000 Polish Jews remained alive from a pre-war population of 3.5 million.

Crushing culture

In October 1939 Joseph Goebbels, Nazi propaganda minister, said 'the Polish nation is not worthy to be called a cultured nation'. Theatres and cinemas were closed (those left open showed German propaganda), museums plundered, existing Polish language newspapers shut down and secondary education curtailed. A year later, the printing of new Polish books was outlawed and in 1943 all Polish books were removed from sale. The country's intelligentsia – the writers, teachers, professors, scientists and lawyers – were dispatched to concentration camps in huge numbers. In common, all areas of Polish culture went underground, where a secretive network of schools, newspapers and theatres achieved a remarkable degree of activity.

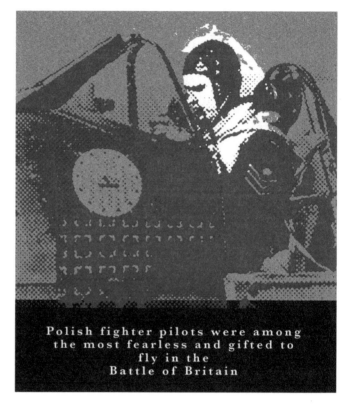

Polish fighter pilots were among the most fearless and gifted to fly in the Battle of Britain

Uprising of 1943, had also failed but was nevertheless the largest single rebellion by the Jews during the Holocaust. Stalin's vision was realised in 1945 when, with Germany defeated, the Yalta Conference placed Poland under Soviet control. The country had been all but destroyed in . the war: a quarter of its population killed; its towns and cities demolished.

A new overlord

Poland lost land to the east, notably Lwów (whose inhabitants were moved en masse to western Poland), after the Second World War, but gained in the west, where the Germans of Silesia were expelled. Gdańsk finally returned to the fold. The country's pre-war

28

multiculturalism was gone; its population now composed almost entirely of ethnic Poles. The rigged elections of 1947 put the Polish Communists in total charge, closely directed by the Politburo in Moscow, and in 1952 the country was renamed the Polska Rzeczpospolita Ludowa (PRL). Any opposition to the authorities, real or imagined, was brutally repressed. Three- and six-year plans got heavy industry moving but failed to collectivise Polish agriculture. After Stalin's death the straitjacket loosened slightly, enough to see strikes and riots in Poznań winning certain concessions in the 'Polish October' of 1956. The promised political reforms didn't materialise, but culturally things improved, and Poland enjoyed a flowering of art, jazz and theatre unrivalled anywhere else in the Eastern Bloc.

It began in the shipyards

The 1960s and '70s were years of tight political control and economic hardship. The Church and the intelligentsia were persecuted, the general population despondent. The announcement of large food price rises stirred unrest. A wave of strikes, demonstrations and rioting broke out in 1970. Government forces – the police and the army – were sent into quell the unrest, resulting in at least 40 deaths and 1,000 injuries. The ensuing outcry saw the longstanding First Secretary of the Polish United Workers' Party, Władysław Gomułka, discredited and he was forced to stand down. An initial improvement in living standards under his successor, Edward Gierek, didn't last– massive price hikes in food brought new protests and strikes, which were brutally subdued. The intelligentsia began to collaborate with workers and an

LECH THEN

The governing Polish United Workers' Party introduced Socialist Realism, or *Socrealizm*, as official policy in 1949, following the Soviet instruction to 'Stalinise' Polish cultural life. Art, music, theatre and architecture were to help create a new social order, or as Stalin said, cultural figures (specifically writers) were the 'engineers of the human soul'. Socialist Realism was shaped begrudgingly into new plays championing the collective society, but left its main legacy in urban planning and architecture (monumental and blocky), in buildings like Warsaw's Palace of Culture and Science and Gdynia railway station. In the visual arts, a Neo-classical Realist style of sculpture and painting rendered industrial workers staring nobly into the distance. The policy was abandoned after Stalin's death.

"YOU WHO
WRONGED A
SIMPLE MAN.
BURSTING INTO
LAUGHTER AT THE
CRIME, DO NOT
FEEL SAFE. THE
POET REMEMBERS.
YOU CAN KILL ONE,
BUT ANOTHER IS
BORN. THE WORDS
ARE WRITTEN
DOWN, THE DEED,
THE DATE."
Inscription by Czesław
Miłosz on a monument
to the 40 Gdańsk
shipyard workers shot
dead by the authorities
whilst protesting about
proposed price rises in
consumer goods in 1970.

LECH NOW

underground network
of opposition grew.
As the economic
situation worsened,
the strikes grew,
focussed increasingly
on the shipyards in
Gdańsk. In 1980,
co-ordinated strikes
(and spontaneous
rioting) led by
Lech Wałęsa, an
electrician at the
Lenin Shipyard of Gdańsk, paralysed the country. Wałęsa,
the strikers and prominent intellectuals were demanding
increased political and social freedom. Gierek relented
and the Gdańsk Agreement was signed, allowing a
federation of trade unions to form across Poland – the
vast collective (soon garnering ten million members) was
called Solidarność (Solidarity). Inevitably, the Kremlin
reacted negatively and stationed tanks along the border
with Poland. Meanwhile in Poland a new leader, General
Jaruzelski, responded to the increasingly debilitating
strikes by imposing martial law in December 1981. All
opposition to the authorities was outlawed and savagely
repressed. Moscow was placated.

Gathering round the Round Table
Martial law ended in 1983, but the opposition movement
in Poland continued to grow, spurred on by the worsening
economic situation. By the late 1980s, amid strikes that
brought the country to a standstill, Jaruzelski agreed to
power-sharing talks. With the reform-minded Mikhail
Gorbachev installed as Soviet leader, the so-called
Round Table talks of 1989 were allowed to proceed.
The outcome was Poland's first democratic election in
decades and a new non-Communist government led by
prime minister Tadeusz Mazowiecki of Solidarność. A
year later, Lech Wałęsa was elected Polish president.

30

1. Identity: the foundations of Polish culture   2. Literature and philosophy   3. Art, architecture and design   4. Music, theatre, and comedy   5. Cinema and fashion   6. Media and communications   7. Food and drink   8. Living culture: the state of modern Poland

Another fresh start

In the years since Poland formed its Third Republic, the country has changed significantly, living through the highs of freedom as well as the subsequent, perhaps inevitable comedown. Dramatic early reforms put food on the shelves but also brought unemployment and inflation, as per the free-market economy standard. Governments came and went with rapidity in the 1990s, and Lech Wałęsa, by general consensus, struggled to manage the early years of a rather fragmentary democracy. Only under President Aleksander Kwaśniewski in the late 1990s did the country begin to stabilise politically and economically – a balancing process that continues today. Kwaśniewski's successor as head of state, Lech Kaczyński, died in a plane crash in 2010. In the wider world, Poland joined NATO in 1999 and five years later signed up enthusiastically to the EU.

The Russian question

Where Poland's post-war relationship with Germany has been one of tentative reconciliation (the thaw began when Polish bishops wrote to their German counterparts ('We forgive and we ask forgiveness') and was then helped along when German chancellor Willy Brandt famously knelt before a monument to the Warsaw Ghetto in 1970), the relationship with Russia is more of a work in progress. Poland and Russia have different accounts of the war: Russia's, to the chagrin of many Poles, remains relatively unapologetic for the invasion of 1939. As recently as 2009, Russia's defence ministry suggested Poland provoked Hitler into starting the war. However, future relations may be more affable. Russia has, after decades, accepted responsibility for the massacre of 20,000 Polish officers at Katyn in 1940, helping to thaw relations, and the two countries are increasingly bound by their agreements over the supply of energy (namely Russian gas to Polish homes).

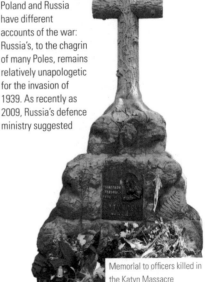

Memorial to officers killed in the Katyn Massacre

1.3 Language and belonging

Language and identity in Poland were buffeted by a turbulent journey through the 20th century. Regional and cultural traditions were suppressed and abused, whilst national identity clung on defiantly to emerge as an important facet of the modern state.

33

1. Identity: the foundations of Polish culture

2. Literature and philosophy

3. Art, architecture and design

4. Music, theatre, and comedy

5. Cinema and fashion

6. Media and communications

7. Food and drink

8. Living culture: the state of modern Poland

We have ways of making you not talk

Under Nazi occupation in the Second World War, signs in Polish were torn down and replaced with Germanised versions, and the use of Polish in public places was banned, including in church services. In the Soviet-occupied sector, the Polish language was officially replaced with Russian or Ukrainian – even the name 'Poland' was banned. After the Second World War, the Soviet restrictions on the Polish language eased somewhat, but Russian was still widely taught in Polish schools.

Kiss or shake?

Generally, the Poles shake hands on greeting, although family members and good friends acknowledge each other with three kisses on alternate cheeks. An old tradition that finds men kissing women on the back of the hand is dying out but is still worth bracing yourself for nonetheless.

Mother tongue: origins and evolution

Polish belongs to the Western Slavic group of languages (alongside Czech and Slovak), and uses the Latin alphabet, albeit incorporating a series of diacritics (the flecks, accents and hooks attached to certain Polish letters that help make the language so impenetrable to the non-speaker).

Like its people, Poland's language has shown remarkable resilience over the centuries. Foreign rulers, notably the Russians and the Germans of the Third Partition, have gone to considerable lengths to crush Polish yet it survives as one of Europe's most intact, homogenous national tongues. The determination of authors and poets to write in the vernacular over the last 500 years certainly helped the language survive, and more recently the country's post-war reconfiguration gave Polish an artificial uniformity (over 96 per cent of the country speaks Polish as a first language) – German-speaking minorities were expelled, whilst a large portion of Poland's ethnic Belarusian and Ukrainian populations ended up outside the realigned borders. The sizeable Jewish community (most of which spoke Polish), resident in the country for centuries, was lost during the war.

Dialects and regional languages

Poland has few distinct regional languages and dialects. There are variances in dialect between the regions, such as between the old kingdoms of Wielkopolska and Małopolska, but the differences are subtle. In the eastern borderlands – the historic *kresy*, as Poles sometimes call the territories that once formed part of the Rzeczpospolita (see section 1.2.2) – the proximity to Lithuania, Belarus, Russia and Ukraine influences the language. Upper Silesia has one of the most divergent Polish dialects – Silesian – spoken by around 60,000 people near the border with the Czech Republic. Silesian has its own TV and radio channels, literature and music, and speakers are pushing to have the dialect officially recognised as a minority language. Further south, the Górale highlanders have a distinct dialect that borrows from the Lemkos, a small ethnic group from the Ukrainian Carpathians. In Pomerania about 50,000 people still speak Kashubian, the only native minority tongue officially recognised by the Polish government as a bona fide language. Like Silesian, Kashubian has its novelists, newspapers and TV channels.

How do the Poles talk?

Despite a deserved reputation for warm welcomes, the Poles are relatively restrained in conversation. An even temperament is important and overt displays of emotion or wild gesticulation are rare, even though they happily stand close to each other whilst talking. Similarly, they talk evenly (even whilst often loud), usually preferring considered response to rapid-fire monologue. Slang is common, and mild swearing may pepper the conversation (although less so with women). In terms of protocol, avoiding eye contact during conversation is considered rude, and whilst topics like religion and abortion are perhaps best avoided on a first meeting, the Poles are generally direct in conversation – they don't skirt around issues, favour allusion or engage in subtle hints.

Polish outside Poland

There are minority Polish-speaking groups in Lithuania, Belarus and Ukraine, particularly in the regions that once fell within the Rzeczpospolita, and significant émigré communities in North America – more than half a million people in the USA use Polish to communicate at home. In Europe, the sheer size and speed of the Polish migration to the UK since Poland's accession to the EU in 2004 (over half a million in the first five years, arriving some 60 years after 200,000 displaced Polish troops settled in the UK under its Polish Resettlement Act) has created pockets of Polish language and culture. In some areas of the UK, employers, particularly in shops, now require some knowledge of Polish from their staff; police forces in the relevant areas have also given out Polish lessons to their personnel.

1.3.2 Being Polish: identity and psyche

'THAT ADVANCED
OUTPOST OF
WESTERN
CIVILISATION.'
Joseph Conrad describes
his homeland

Brand Poland
In 2005 the Polish
Chamber of Commerce
enlisted a British
company, Saffron Brand
Consultants, to help
work on a new brand
identity for Poland.

No longer playing the victim

For generations, poet Adam Mickiewicz' Romantic portrayal of Poland as the 'Christ of Nations', the martyr of Europe, was ingrained in the collective psyche (see section 2.1.4 for more on Mickiewicz), the role confirmed by the prolonged anguish of the 20th century. Poland's fervent Catholicism (with the Church as nation protector) was always closely tied to this identity. However, two decades into the Third Republic this introspection is being assuaged by the confidence of a country finally secure in both its borders and internal affairs (as well, perhaps, as the acceptance that Poland itself has at times been aggressor as well as victim). For all the dislocation the country has endured, the Poles retain the strong patriotism shaped by cultural figures like Chopin and the aforementioned Mickiewicz – although today it's a pragmatic patriotism, aware of the need for co-operation with near neighbours. Similarly, Poland's 'place' in Europe is shifting: whilst the people, ethnic Slavs, may be considered 'Eastern', the country increasingly faces 'West' in attitude and outlook.

Town and country

Each part of Poland has its own characteristics, although the venerable age of the Polish nation and the redistribution of minorities that occurred after the Second World War mean that identity in Poland isn't tied to region in quite the same way that it is in Italy, Spain or Germany. A more distinct sense of identity comes from the contrast between town and country. The slow pace of modernisation in rural Poland (particularly the retention of small, family-run farms) has heightened the sense of disparity with urban Poland, which has changed dramatically over the last 20 years.

Issues with authority

The Poles' relationship with authority has been coloured by its years under Communist rule. Many Poles retain an inherent suspicion of the state – a mistrust heightened by the perceived corruption and instability of the Third Republic's formative years. Similarly, the country still wrestles with itself over the Communist's use of informants and spies. 'Normal' citizens were recruited by the Służba Bezpieczeństwa (SB), the security service, to monitor and report on their fellow Poles in huge numbers, infiltrating every sector of society right through to the final days of the regime (by 1981 the SB had 84,000 informants). Some of these former informants have been publicly 'outed' since the collapse of communism but many – particularly those who worked in positions of authority – have been absorbed into the new system of government.

What are the Poles actually like?

Labelling individuals with national characteristics is always a dangerous business, but it seems fair to say that Poles are polite, easy-going, hospitable people. Indeed, the Russians have sometimes labelled them – with mild disparagement – as 'happy-go-lucky'. Their sense of humour, never far from the surface, has an undercurrent of irony but also a bluntness unhindered by political correctness. For centuries, Poland was one of the most progressive regions in Europe – particularly during the 'golden age' of the Rzeczpospolita – and today, most Poles maintain those egalitarian values. However, the ongoing influence of the Catholic Church also means that Poles can be more puritanical on issues like abortion and gay rights than the citizens of other European nations.

Flying the flag

The Polish flag comprises two horizontal stripes, the white placed above the red. The white comes from the Orzeł Biały (White Eagle), the national coat of arms; the red from the shield against which the eagle is traditionally set. This coat of arms is sometimes set into the flag, although is only done so legally outside Poland. Red and white were chosen as the national colours in 1831 (when Poland wasn't actually a nation state), and the current flag was only officially adopted in 1919. However, the portrayal of a white eagle on a red banner dates back to the 14th century reign of Władysław the Elbow-high.

'I THINK ONE SEES MORE PRETTY WOMEN IN FIVE MINUTES IN WARSAW THAN IN HALF AN HOUR IN ANY OTHER EUROPEAN CAPITAL, LONDON THROWN IN.'
Harry de Windt, 19th century travel writer

2 Literature and philosophy

2.1 Literature

Poland has a long and distinguished literary history. From Middle Age chronicles to rousing Romantic poetry and novels that portrayed the turmoil of the 20th century, Poland itself has frequently been the central character.

2.1.1 A very Polish story

Polish winners of the Nobel Prize in Literature

Henryk Sienkiewicz. Winner in 1905 for *Quo Vadis* (1895).

Władysław Stanisław Reymont. Ennobled in 1924 in recognition of the epic *Chłopi* (1904-09).

Czesław Miłosz. Awarded the prize in 1980 for poetry of "uncompromising clear-sightedness".

Wisława Szymborska. Made a laureate in 1996 for the "ironic precision" of her poetry.

Polish literature has a rich pedigree and yet lacks the international renown it deserves. An apparent preoccupation with domestic affairs may have reduced its ability to travel – as Czesław Miłosz, one of Poland's four Nobel laureates in literature, once noted, the country's literary tradition has been shaped by its own turbulent realities. Where authors elsewhere nurtured fiction, in Poland they were led more often by the fate of the nation and the search for identity.

Today, in quieter times, Polish writers are keen to explore a wide range of subject matter. The literary scene is correspondingly vibrant, especially in the larger cities where events such Kraków's Joseph Conrad Festival and the Wrocław Literature Festival are hugely popular. Alas, whilst those of a literary bent remain fervent about their books, in Poland, as elsewhere, a more general downward trend in adult reading has emerged in recent years. A survey conducted by the Biblioteka Narodowa, Poland's National Library, revealed that even whilst the literacy rate nudges 100 per cent, 56 per cent of the population aged 15 and over didn't open a book in 2010, with the least bookish being the elderly, the unemployed and the less well educated. The same survey also found that 20 per cent of university graduates didn't read books.

If you only ever read five Polish books...

Pan Tadeusz **(1834)**. The national poem no less, as written by Adam Mickiewicz in celebration of his homeland.

Lalka **(1890)**. Love unfurls as Warsaw falls to its knees in a fine socially-aware novel from Bolesław Prus, an author compared with Tolstoy and Dickens.

Sklepy Cynamonowe **(1934)**. Surreal but influential story of life in Drohobycz, a small town in the Polish Ukraine, where the book's author, Bruno Schulz, would later be murdered by the SS.

Zniewolony umysl **(1953)**. Few authors evoked Poland's 20th century suffering quite like poet and essayist Czesław Miłosz. Here he ruminates on one-party rule.

Mała apokalipsa **(1983)**. Covering an agitated day in the life of a washed-up writer, Tadeusz Konwicki's satirical novel was published by the underground press.

Chronicled by clerics

Literature in Poland in the Middle Ages was the preserve of scholarly monks and priests (Poland had adopted Christianity in the 10th century). They wrote in Latin, compiling the lives of saints and liturgical works as well as sprawling histories. Of these chronicles, two in particular stand out: *Chronica seu originale regum et principum Poloniae* (early 13th century), a four-volume history of Poland's kings and princes written by Wincenty Kadłubek, Bishop of Kraków; and Jan Dlugosz' 12-volume *Annales seu cronicae incliti Regni Poloniae* (c.1480), chronicling the 'famous kingdom of Poland'.

Vernacular texts began appearing in the late Middle Ages. The oldest remaining example is the *Kazania świętokrzyskie* (mid 14th century), the *Holy Cross Sermons* that survive in fragments. *Psalterz floriański* (late 14th century) is a translation of the Bible largely in Latin and German but also with some elements of Polish, whilst *Bogurodzica* (c.1407) constitutes a Polish hymn to the Virgin Mary, sung by knights before going into battle. Surviving examples of the *Bogurodzica*, probably the first poem written in Polish, date to the early 15th century, although the verse may be a century older.

Wincenty Kadłubek, Bishop of Kraków

Who's the Daddy? Mikołaj Rej, Jan Kochanowski and the Renaissance

The Renaissance arrived in Poland in the 16th century, somewhat later than elsewhere. Its Humanism (emphasising the dignity of the individual and encouraging the study of classical pagan Latin and Greek texts) combined with the effects of the Reformation and the growing sophistication and wealth of the country's nobility to initiate a 'Golden Age' of Polish literature. Although many works were written in Latin during the Renaissance period, the Polish vernacular would prove itself worthy of being the national literary language. The two leading writers of the Renaissance in Poland were Mikołaj Rej and Jan Kochanowski, both of whom have been credited with being the 'Father of Polish Literature' (no one seems to know who the mother was).

Mikołaj Rej (1505 – 1569)

Pictured with
The Image of a Good Man's Life (1567)

Mikołaj Rej, of noble birth, was widely read in his own lifetime. His influential prose, satirical poems and many epigrams were written exclusively in Polish, partly because – being self-taught – his grasp of Latin was rather shaky. Rej is best known for *Krótka rozprawa między trzema osobami: Panem, Wójtem i Plebanem (A Brief Discussion Between Three Persons: a Squire, a Bailiff and a Parson)* (1543), a satirical verse aimed mainly at the gentry and the clergy. Another Rej work, *Wizerunek własny żywota człowieka poczciwego (A Faithful Image of an Honest Man)* (1558), presents the views of the ideal nobleman (i.e. Rej himself) as laid out in 10,000 lines of prose.

Jan Kochanowski, the son of a country squire, was well schooled in the classics and wrote first in Latin. However, it was his lyric poetry in the vernacular that pushed the Polish Renaissance towards its greatest achievements. His mastery of technique and enthusiasm for his native cultural heritage would influence Polish poetry for generations to come. Some of Kochanowski's *Fraszki (Epigrams)* (1584), a collection of epigrams and poems, such as *Na Lipę (On the Linden Tree)*, are still read by schoolchildren today. His masterpiece was *Treny (Laments)* (1580), comprising 19 elegies about the death of his young daughter, Urszula.

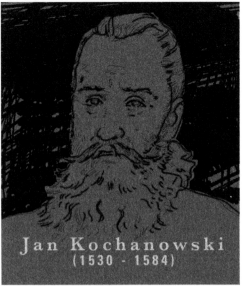

Jan Kochanowski
(1530 - 1584)

Two more Renaissance poets

Klemens Janicki. Janicki left his peasant roots to study in Italy and become one of the most original Latin poets of the 16th century. He's best remembered for *Tristium liber (Book of Sorrows)* (1541), especially *Elegy VII: De se ipso ad posteritatem (About Myself to Posterity)*, in which he foresaw his own death (which duly arrived two years later, with Janicki aged 27).

Szymon Szymonowic. Considered the last great poet of the Polish Renaissance, Szymonowic created an erudite and sympathetic observation of peasant life in Poland in *Sielanki (Pastorals)* (1614).

Two more Renaissance prose writers

Maciej Miechowita. A scholar and geographer known for his *Tractatus de duabus Sarmatiis (Treatise on the Two Sarmatias)* (1517), the first reliable geographical study of Eastern Europe and a work that popularised the myth of Sarmatism – the rather vainglorious (and incorrect) belief that that Polish nobility descended from the ancient Sarmatian tribe.

Piotr Skarga. A Jesuit missionary and preacher whose work in the vernacular, *Żywoty świętych (Lives of the Saints)* (1579), was read widely by his contemporaries and is still in print.

First edition

The first book printed in the Polish language was probably *Raj duszny (Paradise of the soul)* (1513) by Biernat z Lublina. It was a prayer book that was later banned by the Church.

2.1.3 Words of war: the Baroque and the Enlightenment

Three Baroque poets

Mikołaj Sęp Szarzyński. Posthumously published some 20 years after his death, Szarzyński's *Rytmy abo wiersze polskie (Rhythms)* (1601), a collection of melancholic verse, bridged the gap between the Renaissance and the Baroque.

Samuel Twardowski. Author of *Nadobna Paskwalina (Fair Pasqualina)* (1655), the pastoral romance that became a high point of Polish Baroque.

John Andrzej Morsztyn. A courtier and diplomat renowned for his elaborate, extravagant verse, and who took much from the Italian Marinist style, as seen in *Lutnia (Lute)* (1661).

Death and sex in the Baroque

After the achievements of the Renaissance, Poland's literary output in the Baroque period was something of a disappointment. The great optimism of the previous era seemed to now evaporate in a country that was almost constantly at war. Where it did surface, Baroque poetry in Poland – as elsewhere – was characterised by the use of highly ornate language and intricate literary devices, often at the expense of content. Death and earthly delights were prominent themes.

Epics and memoirs

The tumult of Poland's 17th century also ushered in a raft of heroic epic poetry; verse that extolled the victories of the Polish nobility and perpetuated the myth of a glorious Sarmatian ancestry. Waclaw Potocki's *Transakcja wojny chocimskiej (The War of Chocim)* (c.1673), a novel-style verse account of conflict, was a fine example by one of the key Baroque writers. Another poet,

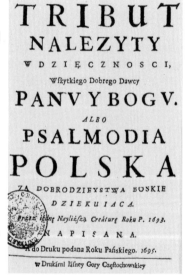

Wespazjan Kochowski, wrote *Psalmodia polska (The Polish Psalmody)* (1695), 36 psalms that gave a quasi-Biblical interpretation of Poland's fate, and which would later influence the Romantic movement.

Memoirs and letters also formed a key element of 17th century Polish literature. The most famous was the vast correspondence between King Jan III Sobieski and his wife, Marie Kazimiera. The royal missives told of their

46

1. Identity: the foundations of Polish culture   **2. Literature and philosophy**   3. Art, architecture and design   4. Music, theatre, and comedy   5. Cinema and fashion   6. Media and communications   7. Food and drink   8. Living culture: the state of modern Poland

personal feelings but also commentated on contemporary events in the later 17th century. *Pamiętniki (Memoirs)* (c.1695), the frequently outrageous recollections of country squire and soldier, Jan Chryzostom Pasek, are perhaps less historically reliable (although eminently readable).

Birth of the novel in Enlightened times

The Enlightenment brought renewed vigour to Polish literature, championed in the later 18th century in particular by King Stanisław II August Poniatowski. Radical reformers wrote didactic treatises, concerning themselves with social and political reform or the nation's cultural heritage. In *O skutecznym rad sposobie (On the Effective Method of Government)* (1760–63), Stanislaw Konarski wrote about ruling, whilst Stanisław Staszic pondered the plight of peasants and workers in the likes of *Przestrogi dla Polski (Warnings for Poland)* (1790). Both were key figures in the Polish Enlightenment.

The foremost poet of the age (indeed the foremost Polish author of the Enlightenment) was Ignacy Krasicki, a bishop with a talent for lyrical wit and elegance. In his *Satyry (Satires)* (1779) he ruminated on human nature and in *Bajki i Przypowieści (Fables and Parables)* (1779), his best known work, created a series of stories that would influence Polish writers for generations to come. Krasicki is also notable for writing the first Polish novel, *Mikołaja Doświadczyńskiego przypadki (The Adventures of Mr. Nicholas Wisdom)* (1776), a utopian fantasy satirising 18th century morality. Novels soon gathered pace as a literary force in Poland, expertly shaped by writers like Jan Potocki, author of *Rękopis znaleziony w Saragossie (The Manuscript Found in Saragossa)* (written in French c.1814 and published in Polish in 1847), framed as a mysterious, recently unearthed manuscript retelling an army officer's adventures amongst thieves, cabbalists and princesses in Spain.

One lump or two? Jan Potocki is a legendary figure in Poland, not least because of his bizarre death. He was a hugely wealthy aristocrat, avid traveller, political activist, alleged member of various secret societies and the first Pole to fly – in a hot air balloon over Warsaw in 1790. Suffering from mental illness in later life, Potocki feared himself transforming into a werewolf. The story goes that he made a silver bullet from the strawberry-shaped knob off his sugar bowl lid, had it blessed by a priest, and then used it to shoot himself in the head.

2.1.4 Born of tragedy: Romantics, Positivists and the Young Poles

Influential friends

Adam Mickiewicz counted Pushkin and Goethe amongst his friends, and translated Byron's *The Giaour* into Polish. He was also the Professor of Literature at the Collège de France, Paris.

Poland looks to its poets

When the Third Partition wiped Poland from the map in 1795, the country's writers reacted with an explosion of creativity. In the early 19th century the Romantic poets emerged with their passionate and accessible language, their patriotism writ large in verse that was inspired by native folklore traditions. These poets became symbols of Poland's very existence; they were seen (and saw themselves) as spiritual leaders and spokesmen for the nation in its quest for independence – particularly after the 1830 uprising, when many pursued their work in exile. A Messianic dimension to literature also emerged in the Romantic period, framing Poland as the 'Christ of nations', destined to suffer for the sins of the world before its inevitable resurrection.

Trzej wieszcze: the Three Bards of Polish Romanticism

Three poets have become associated with Poland's Romantic era, dubbed the Three Bards and recalled with fondness and reverence:

Adam Mickiewicz. Viewed as the greatest of all Polish poets, Mickiewicz stoked the fires of the 19th century independence movement and played a major part in preserving the nation's cultural identity. With *Balady i romanse (Ballads and Romances)* (1822), a collection of sensual love poems and folk tales, he effectively launched Poland's Romantic period. Subsequently,

Adam Mickiewicz
(1798 – 1855)
A Slavonic bard

Mickiewicz lived the life of an archetypal Romantic – he would be imprisoned for patriotic activities and exiled to Russia; he would experience poverty, love affairs and an unhappy marriage to a mentally ill wife; and he would even, it seems, attempt suicide. All of Mickiewicz' work was significant. In *Księgi narodu polskiego i pielgrzymstwa polskiego* (*Books of the Polish Nation and the Polish Pilgrimage*) (1834), a prose history of the nation, he equated the partitioning of Poland to Christ's three days in the tomb. However, it's for his poetry that Mickiewicz is best remembered.

Three Mickiewicz poems

Konrad Wallenrod (1828). A narrative poem depicting the 14th century battles between the Lithuanian people and the knights of the Teutonic Order.

Dziady (*Forefather's Eve*) (1823-1832). This sprawling, mystical poetic drama encompassing folklore, ghosts, tragic love and visions of national independence was written in four parts over a ten-year period.

Pan Tadeusz (*Sir Thaddeus*) (1834). Widely viewed as Mickiewicz' masterpiece, the epic poem tells the story of two feuding noble families in Russian-occupied Lithuania in the early 19th century. *Pan Tadeusz* remains required reading in every Polish school.

Juliusz Słowacki. Słowacki was prolific, writing several poetry dramas and letters (notably the ones to his mother). Having worked briefly for the Polish government during the 1830 Uprising, he was later destined to produce most of his work abroad, notably in Paris. Somewhat underappreciated in his own lifetime, his patriotic verse would prove inspirational and influential to subsequent generations. His major works include *Kordian* (1834), a poetic drama about unrequited love, patriotism and assassination plots; *Anhelli* (1838), a poem in biblical prose depicting the fate of Polish exiles in Siberia; and the unfinished mystical epic *Król-Duch* (*The Spirit King*) (1847).

Zygmunt Krasinski. The third of the great Romantic trio was born in Paris to aristocratic Polish parents, lived much of his life outside Poland and published almost all

The national debt
Adam Mickiewicz is commemorated in statues and monuments all over Poland, the most famous being in Kraków's main market square. Kraków's monument, erected in 1898 on the centenary of the poet's birth, was smashed by the Nazis in 1940. However, the bronze remains were discovered after the war in a scrap metal yard in Hamburg and, in 1955, the statue was restored to its former magnificence. The pedestal bears the inscription '*Adamowi Mickiewiczowi Naród*' – 'For Adam Mickiewicz, from the Nation'.

of his work anonymously. In the poetic drama *Nieboska komedia (The Un-divine Comedy)* (1835), Krasinski addressed class struggle and social revolution, and in *Irydion* (1836) he rendered a tale of oppression and revenge in Ancient Rome. However, he's remembered best for *Przedswit (Before Dawn)* (1843), an influential Messianic poem that inspired with its vision of Poland resurrected.

It's worth noting that the Three Bards also wrote several plays between them, written largely as 'closet dramas' (i.e. for the reader's imaginary stage), even whilst most have been staged at one time or another.

The Fourth Bard?

Cyprian Norwid is regarded by many as being the 'Fourth Bard' of Polish Romanticism. He had a suitably tragic résumé: a polymath of great vision and invention who suffered from poor health, unrequited love, fruitless travels and periods of poverty. He even lived in a graveyard for a while. His work was almost completely ignored during his own lifetime, and his importance only recognised in the early 20th century. *Promethidion* (1851), a verse dialogue on the function of art, and the vast cycle of poems, *Vade-mecum* (1886), are among his best-known works. Norwid died of tuberculosis in 1883 and was buried in a mass grave for Polish paupers in Paris. In 2001 clods of earth from the Parisian burial plot were taken with due symbolism to Wawel Cathedral in Kraków, where Norwid's spirit now lies alongside Adam Mickiewicz and Juliusz Słowacki.

Antoni Malczewski. He only completed one work but it was highly influential: *Maria* (1825), a dark narrative poem about love, murder and suicide.

Aleksander Fredro. Poland's favourite author of comedy wrote social commentary in the Romantic era. *Trzy po trzy (Topsy Turvy Talk)* (1880), published posthumously, was autobiographical. (See section 4.2.2 for Fredro's drama.)

Seweryn Goszczyński. Author of *Zamek kaniowski (The Castle at Kaniow)* (1828), a poetic novel about peasant rebellion and Ukrainian folklore, but perhaps better remembered for a literary attack on Fredro.

Józef Ignacy Kraszewski. The prolific author of over 600 volumes on all sorts of subjects, but best known for historical novels such as *Stara baśń* (1876), set in pre-Christian times.

Narcyza Żmichowska. Female author whose *Poganka (The Pagan Woman)* (1846) and *Biała Róża (The White Rose)* (1861) are seen as early examples of feminist and (obliquely) lesbian literature.

Ryszard Wincenty Berwiński. A respected poet and the author of *Studia o literaturze ludowej* (1854), a study on folk literature.

Joachim Lelewel. The author of many works in prose, including *Polska, dzieje i rzeczy jej rozpatrywane* (1853-76), a history of his homeland in 20 volumes.

Back to reality: 19th century Positivism

In the years after the January Uprising of 1863, so brutally suppressed, writers reacted against the emotive militancy of Romanticism and turned instead to the Positivist movement that advocated a practical, unemotional approach to problem solving. In literature Realism flourished, and with it the evolution of the historical novel. Three writers in particular stood out:

Bolesław Prus. Severely injured as a teenager in the January Uprising, Prus became an agoraphobic journalist in Warsaw who spent his spare time writing Realist novels influenced by the likes of Charles Dickens and Mark Twain. For many, *Lalka (The Doll)* (1890), a sprawling sociological narrative exploring love and social standing, represents Poland's best novel. Another, *Faraon (Pharaoh)* (1897), explored politics and power in Ancient Egypt.

Eliza Orzeszkowa. A campaigner for women's rights and social reform who wrote 30 Positivist-led novels, the

"THE AIM OF LITERATURE IS TO AID THE SPIRITUAL DEVELOPMENT OF THE INDIVIDUAL AND OF SOCIETY."
Bolesław Prus

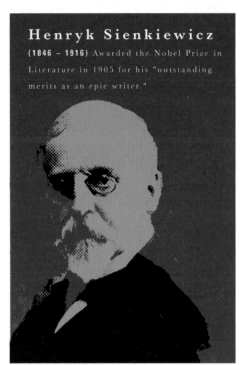

Henryk Sienkiewicz
(1846 – 1916) Awarded the Nobel Prize in
Literature in 1905 for his "outstanding
merits as an epic writer."

most successful of which, *Nad
Niemnem (On the Banks of the
Niemen)* (1887), charted the
struggles of the Polish nobility after
the January Uprising.

Henryk Sienkiewicz. One of
Poland's most esteemed writers,
Sienkiewicz was the author of
several historical novels. He
wrote a famous trilogy – *Ogniem
i mieczem (With Fire and Sword)*
(1884), *Potop (The Deluge)* (1886)
and *Pan Wołodyjowski (Pan
Michael)* (1888) – that dramatised
Poland's turbulent journey through
the 17th century. Another novel,
Quo Vadis (1895), set in Nero's
Ancient Rome, brought international fame and earned the
author the 1905 Nobel Prize in Literature, given "for his
outstanding merits as an epic writer".

The enthusiasm of youth

The inherently calming qualities of Positivism were
cast aside in the late 19th century as authors once again
sought a more proactive response to Poland's ongoing
occupation by foreign powers. The Młoda Polska – Young
Poland – movement (see section 1.2.3) emerged, bringing
writers from a variety of backgrounds together in a loose
collective keen to reintroduce emotion and imagination
into literature, and to draw the impetus away from what
they regarded as a slumbering intelligentsia. It was a
Modernist movement that ranged across the genres,
encompassing the visual arts, music and literature, in
which there were various figures of note:

Jan Kasprowicz. Born of peasant stock, Kasprowicz
became a prolific translator of foreign literature, but was
also a well respected poet in his own right, penning the

1. Identity: the
foundations
of Polish culture

**2. Literature
and philosophy**

3. Art, architecture
and design

4. Music, theatre,
and comedy

5. Cinema
and fashion

6. Media and
communications

7. Food and drink

8. Living culture:
the state of
modern Poland

likes of *Ginącemu światu (To a Dying World)* (1901), in which he addresses the sufferings of mankind.

Stefan Żeromski. A novelist who displayed great social conscience in powerful, poetic works including *Ludzie bezdomni (Homeless People)* (1900), which dealt with social work among the poor, and *Wierna rzeka (The Faithful River)* (1912), about a soldier wounded in the January Uprising.

Władysław Stanisław Reymont. Despite humble origins, Reymont achieved great fame for his highly readable Realist novels. *Ziemia Obiecana (The Promised Land)* (1899), a saga set around a factory, was widely lauded, but he is perhaps best remembered for *Chłopi (The Peasants)* (1904-09), the four-volume epic about contemporary peasant life for which he was awarded the 1924 Nobel Prize in Literature.

A Pole apart: Joseph Conrad

The final years of the 19th century found another young Pole changing the face of modern literature, albeit after leaving his homeland behind. Józef Teodor Konrad Korzeniowski came from patriotic Polish noble stock but left Poland at the age of 16 for a life on the high seas, having been orphaned five years earlier. Eventually he settled in England, changed his name to Joseph Conrad and took British citizenship. Conrad wrote all of his novels and short stories in English – his third language (after Polish and French) – drawing upon his experiences of travel in works like *The Nigger of the 'Narcissus'* (1897), which relayed the fate of a black sailor on a voyage from Bombay to London. In *Lord Jim* (1900), Conrad wrote about the adventures of a British sailor with a shameful past, and in his best-known work, *Heart of Darkness* (1899), created a novella in which the impenetrable African jungle reflected the human heart. Conrad's powerful and precise language, and his scrutiny of the human condition, would influence many writers to come.

Conrad comes home

For years, Joseph Conrad – having left Kraków as a teenager, become a British citizen and chosen to write in English – occupied a rather uncertain place in the pantheon of Polish literature. However, more recently the author has been reclaimed by the country of his birth. In 2009 Kraków staged its first Conrad Festival, a now annual event featuring writers from Poland and beyond.

JÓZEF KONRAD KORZENIOWSKI
PISARZ

2.1.5 Literature in a time of tyranny:
the 20th century

In memory of Bruno

Bruno Schulz wasn't just a literary talent; he was also an accomplished artist. When his hometown, Drohobycz (now in Ukraine), fell under German occupation in 1941, it seems Schulz enjoyed a degree of protection from Gestapo officer Felix Landau, given in return for painting murals in Landau's temporary home. However, Schulz, a Jew, was later killed by another Nazi officer, Karl Günther, as payback for Landau's murder of a Jewish dentist under Günther's protection. The murals, depicting a series of eerie fairytale characters, became lost – some questioned if they'd ever existed – until they were rediscovered in 2001 by a German filmmaker, Benjamin Geissler. Parts of the mural were removed and taken to Yad Vashem, Jerusalem's Holocaust Museum, during restoration, initiating a seven-year diplomatic tug of war with the Ukrainian authorities. The dispute was settled in 2008; Israel accepted that the paintings belonged to Ukraine, and Yad Vashem was allowed to keep its pieces on a long-term loan.

Let freedom ring, albeit briefly

When Poland regained its sovereignty in 1918, having waited 123 years, the newfound atmosphere of freedom nurtured a wide variety of literary styles and themes. Poetry, having receded into the novel's shadow during the Positivist years, found renewed vigour. Julian Tuwim wrote highly emotional lyric poetry in 'real' language as a member of the Skamander group, an experimental clique keen to shed Polish poetry's traditional patriotic function in favour of more everyday themes. His acclaimed *Biblia cyganska (The Gypsy Bible)* (1933) was typical. Another poet from another clique, Julian Przybos of the Kraków Avantgarde group, mirrored the techniques being used by the Italian Futurists, as seen in works like *Śruby (Screws)* (1925). A third, Bolesław Leśmian, used folklore and erotic imagery in highly regarded Expressionist poetry, at its finest in *Napój cienisty (The Shadowy Drink)* (1936).

Three important novelists from the interwar period

Witold Gombrowicz. A novelist and dramatist whose first novel, *Ferdydurke* (1937), the disturbing story of a grown man transformed into a teenager, is now viewed (after decades of relative anonymity) as a masterpiece of European Modernism. Gombrowicz left Poland for Argentina before the Second World War, remaining in South America until the early 1960s. He wrote further significant novels, including *Pornografia* (1960), the tale of murder and sexual manipulation in wartime Poland, although only achieved fame in later life.

Stanisław Ignacy Witkiewicz. Known primarily as a playwright (see section 4.2.3), Witkiewicz also authored three novels (and also found time to paint), of which *Nienasycenie (Insatiability)* (1930), a complex vision of decadence under a totalitarian regime, is the best known.

Bruno Schulz. A Jewish writer and artist born in Drohobycz in Polish Ukraine, where he lived most of his life and where he was murdered by a Nazi officer in

1942. Schulz is regarded as one of the greatest and most original writers of the 20th century. He left a tragically small body of work – namely *Sklepy Cynamonowe (The Cinnamon Shops)* (1934) and *Sanatorium Pod Klepsydrą (Sanatorium Under the Sign of the Hourglass)* (1937) – in which he created fantastic, surreal settings for tales of everyday life and death in a small town.

Grim calm after the storm

The Holocaust and its aftermath proved strong themes in post-war literature, and two writers in particular rendered the horror of Poland's war years in prose. Zofia Nałkowska wrote *Medaliony* (*Medallions*) (1946), a collection of eight stories based on evidence given by the victims and witnesses of Nazi atrocities in Poland to an investigation committee of which the author was a member. Tadeusz Borowski wrote two books, *Pożegnanie z Marią (Farewell to Maria)* (1948) and *Kamienny świat* (*The World of Stone*) (1948), published collectively in English as *This Way for the Gas, Ladies and Gentlemen* (1967). Each of the stories within drew on the author's experiences of Auschwitz, portraying not only the brutality of the guards, but also the tension and duplicity between inmates. A third author, Jerzy Andrzejewski, wrote *Popiół i diament (Ashes and Diamonds)* (1948), a much read novel that captured the conflicts between Polish patriots and the Communist authorities in the last days of the war.

No happy ending

Król Maciuś Pierwszy (King Matt the First) (1923) is a famous Polish children's book. It relates the adventures of a boy who becomes king and tries unsuccessfully to give extra rights (and chocolate) to children. The story's creator, Janusz Korczak, a paediatrician by trade, lost his life in the Holocaust. Korczak was working at an orphanage in the Warsaw Ghetto in 1942 when German soldiers arrived to take the children away to Treblinka extermination camp. The author's fame gave him the opportunity to save himself, yet he decided to go with the children – nearly 200 in all – leading them through the streets of Warsaw, dressed in their best clothes, on their final journey. Korczak died soon after his arrival at the camp.

Tadeusz Borowski, author of the acclaimed *This Way for the Gas, Ladies and Gentlemen,* was sent to Auschwitz as a political dissident. He survived and went on to work as a journalist after the war. Initially he was a staunch supporter of the Communist regime but in 1951, perhaps disillusioned with the authorities (no one really knows), he committed suicide, aged 28, by asphyxiating himself in the kitchen oven. He died only three days after the birth of his daughter.

"A VOYAGE TO THE LIMIT OF A PARTICULAR EXPERIENCE." Tadeusz Borowski describes his stories of Auschwitz

Socialist Realism and the second circulation

The Communist regime was suffocating Polish literature by the late 1940s, encouraging many of the country's emerging writers – authors like Czesław Miłosz (of whom more later) – to flee the country. Those who remained were expected to work within the confines of Socialist Realism, extolling the virtues of life in Stalin's brave new world and contributing to the Sovietisation of Polish culture.

Despite the cultural thaw that followed Stalin's death, Polish authors remained subject to the state's capricious and unpredictable censorship in the later 1950s. Most proscribed publications were smuggled in from abroad, although a small but significant underground press, the 'second circulation' as it was known, began to gather momentum in the mid 1970s, offering a platform to authors critical of the regime. Satirical novelist Tadeusz Konwicki found a readership via the clandestine presses of the second circulation. He wrote *Kompleks polski (The Polish Complex)* (1977), examining Poland's past and present and *Mała apokalipsa (A Minor Apocalypse)* (1979), in which a disillusioned writer is asked to set himself on fire in front of the Palace of Culture and Science, the Soviet-era building given as a gift to Poland by the USSR and which still dominates the Warsaw skyline (see section 3.2.3 for more).

Four outstanding post-war Polish writers
Despite the creative restraints imposed on Polish writers
in the years of Soviet rule, a handful of internationally
renowned poets and novelists emerged:

Zbigniew Herbert. A former member of the Armia
Krajowa resistance movement and one of Poland's most
beloved 20th century poets, Herbert travelled widely to
escape the constraints of the Communist government
although remained passionate about his country's fate.
Indeed, in the 1980s he became closely identified with
the Solidarity movement. Herbert's acclaimed collections
of verse, including *Pan Cogito (Mr. Cogito)* (1974) and
*Raport z oblężonego miasta i inne wiersze (Report from
the Besieged City)* (1983), employed compassion, irony
and classical allusion in their attempts to bring some
order to the discord of life in 20th century Poland, or as
Herbert called it "the treasure house of all misfortune".

Wisława Szymborska. Having adhered initially to the
precepts of Socialist Realism, Szymborska's poetry
adopted a more personal slant in the later 1950s. For
decades she dealt with everyday emotions and issues
using concise, deceptively simple language in collections
such as *Wołanie do Yeti (Calling Out to Yeti)* (1957), and
Widok z ziarnkiem piasku (View with a Grain of Sand)
(1996). One particular poem, *Kot w pustym mieszkaniu
(Cat in an Empty Apartment)* (1993), became hugely
popular. Szymborska's status as a national treasure was
confirmed in 1996 with the award of the Nobel Prize in
Literature, given "for poetry that with ironic precision
allows the historical and biological context to come to
light in fragments of human reality".

1. Identity: the
foundations
of Polish culture   **2. Literature
and philosophy**   3. Art, architecture
and design   4. Music, theatre,
and comedy   5. Cinema
and fashion   6. Media and
communications   7. Food and drink   8. Living culture:
the state of
modern Poland

Stanisław Lem. Lem's intelligent, darkly humorous
science fiction novels have garnered international
attention, finding translation in over 40 languages. *Głos
Pana (His Master's Voice)* (1968) was one of his best,
detailing the futile efforts of scientists in the Nevada
desert to decode what may be a message from outer
space. Similarly, *Solaris* (1961), in which a space station
tries and fails to communicate with the eponymous
distant planet covered by a living, intelligent ocean, was
an international bestseller. *Solaris* has been adapted for
the screen twice, filmed by both Andrei Tarkovsky (1972)
and Steven Soderbergh (2002). Another Lem work, *Roly
Poly*, a short story about organ transplantation, was made
into a film for TV by Andrzej Wajda (1968).

Czesław Miłosz. The poetry and prose of Czesław
Miłosz, banned for many years in Poland, have accorded
the author a towering status in the story of Polish
literature. The best of his early poetry, *Ocalenie (Rescue)*
(1945) was written during the Second World War, after
which he worked briefly as a cultural attaché for the
Communist authorities. Having defected to France in
1951, Miłosz produced his finest work in exile, notably
in the USA where he took up citizenship in 1970. He
explored spiritual and political concerns using precise
free verse in work such as *Traktat poetycki (Treatise on
Poetry)* (1957), inspired by Polish history, and *Miasto bez
imienia (The City Without a Name)* (1969), a journey of
memory, recounted during a trip through Death Valley.
However, Miłosz is perhaps best known for *Zniewolony
umysł (The Captive Mind)* (1953), a collection of essays

1. Identity: the
foundations
of Polish culture

**2. Literature
and philosophy**

3. Art, architecture
and design

4. Music, theatre,
and comedy

5. Cinema
and fashion

6. Media and
communications

7. Food and drink

8. Living culture:
the state of
modern Poland

examining the complex nature of totalitarianism. Having won the Nobel Prize in Literature in 1980, Miłosz returned to Poland after the fall of Communism to a hero's welcome. He died in Kraków in 2004, aged 93.

Poland in dispatches

Whilst Herbert, Miłosz and co vocalised Poland's plight using metaphor and simile, other writers were more direct, employing non-fiction literature to recount theirs and their country's experiences under Communist rule. Kazimierz Brandys, co-founder of the underground journal *Zapis* in the 1970s, published his excellent diaries in English as *A Warsaw Diary*, 1978–1981 (1983), whilst reportage journalist Ryszard Kapuściński looked to conflict elsewhere with *Wojna futbolowa* (*The Soccer War*) (1978), detailing the brief war between Honduras and El Salvador.

Czesław Miłosz
(1911 – 2004)

Poland's post-Communist literary scene has developed with vibrancy and optimism. Today, it's characterised by its diversity, its writers no longer bound by censorship nor the attendant obligation to rebuke its perpetrators. Like the rest of the Western world, the contemporary Polish literary canon now features historical fiction, crime and mystery, science fiction and serious 'literary' novels.

Popular contemporary authors, a selection
Andrzej Sapkowski. Well known for a series of fantasy novels, *Saga o Wiedźminie (Witcher Saga)* (1994-1999).

Marek Krajewski. The grimy pre-war Breslau (now Wrocław) world of policeman Eberhard Mock has featured in five crime fiction novels by Krajewski. *Widma w mieście Breslau (Phantoms in Breslau)* (2005) was a bestseller.

Michał Witkowski. The author of well-received gay fiction, including *Lubiewo (Lovetown)* (2005).

Janusz Leon Wisniewski. Enjoyed a huge hit with the novel *S@motność w Sieci (Loneliness on the Net)* (2001), a love story played out in the Internet age.

Mariusz Szczygieł. A non-fiction author who impressed with *Gottland* (2008), an award-winning study of the Czechs under Communism.

Hanna Krall. Krall has made the wartime relationship between Poles and Jews a central theme; *Zdążyć przed Panem Bogiem (Shielding the Flame)* (1977) was based on an interview with a leader of the Warsaw Uprising

Five great works of modern literary fiction

Weiser Dawidek *(Who was David Weiser?)* (1987). The debut novel by Paweł Huelle centred on the quest to discover the truth about a mysterious Jewish schoolboy.

Opowieści galicyjskie *(Tales of Galicia)* (1995). A fictional travelogue featuring some very strange characters, from the pen of Andrzej Stasiuk.

Pod mocnym aniołem *(The Mighty Angel)* (2000). Jerzy Pilch's drinking culture novel about a third-generation alcoholic won the NIKE award in 2001.

Wojna polsko-ruska pod flagą biało-czerwoną *(White and Red)* (2002). The first novel by Dorota Masłowska, published when she was 19, was the brutally realistic story of a lowlife speed freak.

Bieguni (2007). Olga Tokarczuk's episodic story of modern nomads (or 'runners') from one of Poland's most acclaimed contemporary authors; *Bieguni* was the 2008 NIKE winner.

The NIKE

The *Nagroda Literacka* (NIKE) Literary Award, founded in 1997 and held every October, is presented for the best Polish book by a living author from the previous year. It is Poland's most prestigious literary award, chosen by a select jury of leading literary types. Another NIKE award, organised by the *Gazeta Wyborcza* newspaper, is selected by the audience.

2.2 Philosophy

Copernicus aside, Poland doesn't boast a raft of internationally famous philosophers in the way that France or Germany does. However, the country has always had a rich seam of intellectual life, nurturing thinkers who helped the country plot a course through troubled times.

2.2.1 From Witelo to Copernicus

Middle Ages spread: developing a taste for plurality
The first Polish philosopher of note was Witelo, a 13th century mathematician, physicist and philosopher of Thuringian/Polish stock, known for his *Perspectivorum libri decem (Ten Books of Optics)* (c.1273), a work that dealt with optics, the metaphysics of light and the psychology of perception.

Two centuries after Witelo, the Kraków Academy (now the Jagiellonian University) became a hub for progressive thought. The predominant philosophical school was Scholasticism, which took a rigorously academic approach to its studies reconciling the Christian faith with Ancient Greek reason, particularly Aristotle's works in Logic, Metaphysics and Ethics. Philosophers such as Jan z Głogowa, Michał Falkener and Benedykt Hesse wrote treatises on the prevalent currents of thought, based in particular on Thomism (the Aristotelian teachings of St. Thomas Aquinas) and Ockhamist philosophy (inspired by William of Ockham).

The 15th century heyday of the Kraków Academy introduced an enduring taste for pluralism into Polish philosophy. Ever since, the country's key thinkers have been keen to acknowledge different standpoints and to reconcile them with existing schools of thought. It's an approach that has borne some works of great learning, if not a particularly strong tradition of original thought. Another abiding – and perhaps more fruitful – trait of Polish philosophy has been scholars' interest in politics. *Tractatus de potestate papae et imperatoris respectu infidelium (Treatise on the Power of the Pope and the Emperor over the Infidels)* (1415), written by Paweł Włodkowic, set the tone. Włodkowic argued that all necessary measures are justifiable if a country is required to defend itself against a foreign aggressor, and that Christian and non-Christian nations should have the right to live in peace. This moderating, tolerant voice would become important to Polish political and philosophical thought in the years ahead.

Stoic about the Renaissance

While Polish thought remained largely Scholastic during the country's 16th century encounter with the Renaissance, Stoicism (in which virtue is the only happiness and all passions are eliminated) also emerged and grew in influence. Two thinkers stood out, both professors at the Kraków Academy:

Jakub Górski sought to reconcile Stoicism with the works of Aristotle in *Commentariorum artis dialecticae libri decem (Ten Books of Commentaries on the Dialectical Art)* (1562).

Adam Burski wrote *Dialectica Ciceronis (The Dialectics of Cicero)* (1604), singing the praises of Stoic empiricism, which maintained that 'sense-perception' was the source of knowledge.

Democratic ideals

Political philosophy also developed in the Renaissance. Andrzej Frycz Modrzewski, sometimes referred to as the 'father of Polish democracy', gained international acclaim with the *Commentariorum de republica emendanda libri quinque (Commentaries on Reforming the State in Five Books)* (1551), which called for the radical reform of state and Church (much to their dismay), and the adoption of a political system based on equality before the law for all citizens. Another political philosopher, Wawrzyniec Goślicki, a diplomat and bishop, wrote *De optimo senatore (The Accomplished Senator)* (1568). The influential work demanded a senate to represent the people and to regulate the monarchy.

Man on the moon

Witelo has never been a household name exactly but he was respected enough in some circles to merit an eponymous crater on the Moon. If you want to look for it, the Vitello Crater is on the southern edge of the Sea of Moisture (the Mare Humorum).

Legend has it that
as Copernicus lay
unconscious on his
deathbed following a
stroke, a copy of *De
revolutionibus orbium
coelestium*, only just
published, was placed in
his hands. He opened his
eyes long enough to see
his earth-shattering book
before passing away.

Get over yourselves, you're not the centre of the universe

The most significant Polish contribution to philosophical thought in the 16th century was made by Mikołaj Kopernik, aka Nicolaus Copernicus (like many of his contemporaries, Mikołaj felt the Latinised version of his name carried greater cachet). Although Copernicus is often regarded primarily as an astronomer, *De revolutionibus orbium coelestium (On the Revolutions of the Heavenly Spheres)* (printed in 1543, the year of his death) had its roots in philosophy, especially the writings of Plato, and encouraged intellectuals to question everything that had gone before. He rejected Ptolemy's geocentric (Earth-centred) model of the universe, proposing instead a heliocentric (Sun-centred) theory.

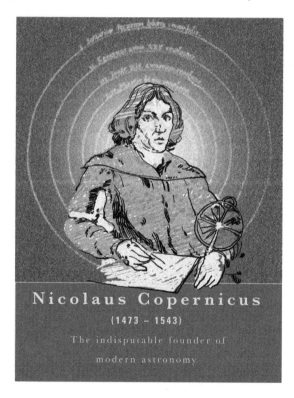

Nicolaus Copernicus

(1473 – 1543)

The indisputable founder of

modern astronomy

1. Identity: the
foundations
of Polish culture

**2. Literature
and philosophy**

3. Art, architecture
and design

4. Music, theatre,
and comedy

5. Cinema
and fashion

6. Media and
communications

7. Food and drink

8. Living culture:
the state of
modern Poland

2.2.2 Shaping a national philosophy: the Enlightenment, the Messianics and the Positivists

In the plural: two Enlightenment theories are better than one

In the hundred years before the Enlightenment gathered pace, Poland's stumbling progress through a series of military and political crises didn't encourage great leaps forward in progressive thought. One figure, Sebastian Petrycy, a philosopher and physician, did make an impact in the early 17th century with the first Polish translation of Aristotle's collected works, but the country's isolation from foreign ideas prevented much else of note from emerging.

However, as the Enlightenment took hold in the 18th century new ideas flooded into Poland. Kantianism, which suggested that only experienced phenomena can be known and noumena (the world of ideas) are completely unknowable 'things in themselves' to the human mind, and Scottish Common Sense Realism – from Thomas Reid et al. who argued that there are certain principles in life, such as the existence of the external world, that an individual is led to believe and must take for granted without being able to explain them – were particularly influential. As was their pluralist wont, Polish philosophers like Jędrzej Śniadecki attempted to reconcile these new schools of thought.

Śniadecki's brother, Jan, became the most important Polish philosopher of the Enlightenment. He developed a version of Positivism, the concept that knowledge is based on sense and positive verification, and became well known as the author of *O rachunku losów* (*On the Calculation of Chance*) (1817) and *Filozofia umysłu ludzkiego* (*The Philosophy of the Human Mind*) (1821). The political philosophy of Stanisław Staszic and Hugo Kołłątaj was also of importance to the Enlightenment. Both were priests and both championed radical reform. They wrote extensively on social duty and morality – Staszic in *Ród Ludzki* (*The Human Race*) (1820) and Kołłątaj in *Porządek fizyczno-moralny* (*The Physical-Moral Order*) (1810).

Józef of all trades

Józef Hoene-Wroński was a busy eccentric, engaging with the great (and not so great) issues of the day when he wasn't writing Messianic and mathematically led philosophy. Working as an émigré in Paris, he spent a good portion of his time writing to European leaders offering complex mathematical formulae to help them govern. He was also an inventor of sorts: devising caterpillar-like vehicles to compete with trains; attempting to build a 'prognometre', a device to predict the future; and drawing up plans for a perpetual motion machine. Inevitably, most of his inventions – along with his theories – underwhelmed, and he died poor and somewhat unloved.

Deifying Poland

The Third Partition of 1795 and failed November Uprising of 1830 gave rise to Messianism, a loose term coined for the philosophies whose protagonists felt themselves charged with saving mankind. August Cieszkowski accorded the Slavic peoples in general a special role in bringing about heaven on earth, explaining all in *Ojcze Nasz* (*Our Father*) (1848). Others, such as poet Adam Mickiewicz (see section 2.1.4 for more) saw Poland specifically as the martyred 'Christ of Nations'. For the eccentric mathematician, inventor and thinker Józef Hoene-Wroński, philosophy itself was the messiah.

The Positivist backlash

Not all 19th century Polish philosophers concerned themselves with Messianism. Some, such as Michał Wiszniewski, had more Positivist leanings. Wiszniewski wrote pioneering works on psychology, including *Charaktery rozumów ludzkich* (*Characters of Human Minds*) (1837). Later in the century, after the crushing defeat of the 1863 January Uprising and the attendant reprisals, Messianism was more heavily criticised as irresponsible and a new realistic Positivism emerged, stressing the importance of reform and hard work. The main representatives were Adam Mahrburg and Julian Ochorowicz. Mahrburg became the outstanding figure amongst the Polish Positivists, the author of influential works including *Teoria celowości ze stanowiska naukowego (The Theory of Purpose From a Scientific Standpoint)* (1888).

1. Identity: the foundations of Polish culture

2. Literature and philosophy

3. Art, architecture and design

4. Music, theatre, and comedy

5. Cinema and fashion

6. Media and communications

7. Food and drink

8. Living culture, the state of modern Poland

2.2.3 Maths and Marxism:
philosophy in the modern era

Twardowski and the Lwów-Warsaw School

New modes of thought sparked into life in the late 19th and early 20th centuries, led in particular by Kazimierz Twardowski, a teacher of the University of Lwów and later in Warsaw. He championed analytic philosophy and mathematical logic, stressing the primacy of scientific methods over speculative systems for problem solving. Duly dubbed the 'father of contemporary Polish philosophy', Twardowski established the Lwów-Warsaw School, perhaps the single most significant clique in the history of Polish philosophy. Typically, the protagonists were pluralist in nature, keen to explore all areas of philosophy even whilst the school was defined by an analytical approach. The school bore the country's most significant 20th century thinkers before its demise in the Second World War:

Kazimierz Twardowski

Jan Łukasiewicz. A key proponent of mathematical logic, known for developing the three-valued propositional calculus, introduced in 1917, in which he expanded upon the traditional Aristotelian view that there are only two possible truth values – 'true' or 'false' – for any logical proposition (e.g. all men are mortal), by adding a third: 'undetermined'.

Did you write the book of love?

Any inventory of significant 20th century Polish philosophers could include Karol Wojtyła. He wrote *Miłość i odpowiedzialność* (1960), published in English as *Love and Responsibility* (1981), a philosophical, psychological and theological analysis of love. This work, and others by Wojtyła, grew in popularity after his election as Pope John Paul II in 1978.

Puppy love for the party
Like many of his contemporaries, from authors to artists and philosophers, Leszek Kołakowski initially embraced Communist ideology. In the years immediately after the Second World War (during which he was expelled with his mother from Lodz after the Gestapo killed his father), Kołakowski joined the Polish United Workers' Party. However, a trip to Stalin's Moscow in the early 1950s brought disillusionment and a repositioning towards 'Marxist humanism'. A speech attacking the government led to his expulsion from the party in 1966 and, two years later, his dismissal from a teaching post at Warsaw University. He fled to the USA, renounced Marxism altogether and saw his work banned in Poland for the next 20 years. However, underground publishers in Poland continued to circulate Kołakowski's writing, some of which inspired the nascent Solidarity movement.

Stanisław Leśniewski. An influential advocate of logical systems, notably his concept of 'mereology', which examined the relation between part and whole. Leśniewski attempted to solve the problems of Set Theory, as per the Barber Paradox (does the barber who shaves all the men in town who do not shave themselves shave himself?) by viewing the whole as a concrete class physically composed of its parts.

Tadeusz Kotarbiński. A philosopher best remembered for his theory of 'reism', which postulates that all abstract concepts can be reduced to concrete objects, as detailed in *Elementy teorii poznania, logiki formalnej i metodologii nauk* (1929).

Alfred Tarski. A pupil of Leśniewski, Tarski was a world-renowned logician and analytical philosopher. His famous (and highly complex) 1933 paper *Pojęcie prawdy w językach nauk dedukcyjnych (The Concept of Truth in the Languages of Deductive Sciences)* set out a mathematical definition of truth in formal languages.

Pre-war phenomena
Poland's pre-war years of independence also nourished an interest in phenomenology, the study of experienced phenomena free from conceptual presuppositions. It was a doctrine established by Austrian-born Edmund Husserl, but the key representative of phenomenology in Poland was Roman Ingarden, whose own particular version was set out in *Spór o istnienie świata (Controversy Over the Existence of the World)* (1948).

State-spun philosophies and the dissidents
Inevitably, Poland's post-war leaders attempted to package Marxism as the only admissible philosophy going. However, true to their pluralist heritage, the country's intelligentsia treated it as only one of many schools to be considered. Even the likes of Adam Schaff, a state-sanctioned Marxist thinker, incurred the

authorities' rancour on the publication of *Marksizm a jednostka ludzka (Marxism and the Human Individual)* (1965), in which he argued that the alienation of the individual was entirely possible in a Socialist society.

Others, living outside Poland, were openly critical of the regime. Leszek Kołakowski's became an enduringly dissident voice; in the esteemed *Główne nurty marksizmu (Main Currents of Marxism)* (1976) he maintained that Stalinism was the logical end result of Marxism. Another figure, Józef Tischner, a priest, became known for the 'philosophy of drama' that explored truth and freedom, as expressed in works such as *Spór o istnienie człowieka (The Controversy over Human Existence)* (1998). Tischner is also remembered for his association with the Solidarity movement, for which he became the unofficial chaplain and moral spokesman. He wrote about his Solidarity experiences in *Etyka Solidarności (The Spirit of Solidarity)* (1981).

Plurality persists

In post-Communist Poland, philosophy retains its diverse, pluralistic character. Phenomenology, first explored in the antebellum period, remains an important force, developed by figures like Anna-Teresa Tymieniecka (resident in the USA), who wrote *Equipoise in the Life-Strategies of Reason* (2000). Similarly, Catholic philosophy has also had its advocates, not least Józef Życiński, the one-time archbishop of Lublin and author of *Bóg i ewolucja (God and Evolution)* (2002), a work that explored the relationship – and potential harmony – between Christian religion and evolutionary theory.

"A MODERN PHILOSOPHER WHO HAS NEVER ONCE SUSPECTED HIMSELF OF BEING A CHARLATAN MUST BE SUCH A SHALLOW MIND THAT HIS WORK IS PROBABLY NOT WORTH READING."
Leszek Kołakowski.

3 Art, architecture and design

3.1 Art and design

For centuries, art in Poland was dominated by foreigners working under the patronage of Church and state. Only amid the distress of occupation and partition did homegrown talent emerge to shape a Polish mode of art, drawing the attention of an international audience with its impassioned Romanticism.

3.1.1 Sacred at heart: art before the Romantics

It began with interior design

When Mieszko I adopted Christianity on Poland's behalf in 966, monastic orders arrived from France, Germany and Belgium and introduced Western styles of art and decoration. In particular, they decorated the interiors of Romanesque monasteries and churches; the work almost certainly carried out by foreign artists and craftsmen. A handful of Romanesque interiors have survived the intervening centuries. At the Church of the Holy Trinity in Strzelno, for example, a pair of late 12th century stone columns adorned with 36 carved figures representing the Virtues and Vices remain in place, having been rediscovered during restoration work in 1946. And in Gniezno, in the old Piast heartland of Wielkopolska, the cathedral's bronze doors represent Poland's finest surviving slice of pre-Gothic craftsmanship. Created some time around 1175, the doors are decorated with 18 scenes in relief, each depicting an episode in the life or death of Saint Adalbert, whose remains were purchased by King Bolesław I Chrobry from the Prussians for their weight in gold. Gniezno's doors are duly regarded as the first Polish work of art with a national theme.

The doors at Gniezno Cathedral

Art remained mostly sacred in nature through to the 14th and 15th centuries. As Gothic superseded Romanesque as a building style, the sculpture and painting used to decorate the country's churches became more sophisticated, the figures and their garments increasingly realistic. However, such work remained the domain of foreign artists.

Art steps outside the Church

As the Renaissance spread north from Italy in the 16th century, Polish art became more diverse. The preoccupation with religious decoration continued with sculpture, illuminated manuscripts and wall paintings, such as *Ukrzyżowanie* (*Crucifixion*) (1530-41), daubed on the walls of Mogiła's Cistercian Abbey by Stanisław Samostrzelnik, the Kraków monk who led the way in Renaissance Polish art. However, new patrons began to emerge outside the church, not least at the royal court in Kraków (the hub for Polish culture at the time) and amongst nobles in search of a portrait. Secular art duly began to flourish. Foreign artists like Hans Dürer and Hans Süss, both German, remained important, but a major Polish contribution came from Marcin Krober, the Wrocław court painter whose portrait of *Anna Jagiellonka* (1595) was particularly lauded for its psychological depth.

Italian imports in the Baroque

The dramatic light, colour and technical excellence of Baroque lent itself well to the demands of Church and nobility in 17th century Poland. Grand palaces, churches and castles were adorned with sculpture, stucco and wall paintings, most of which were produced by Italians resident in Poland – the likes of Clemente Molli (sculptor), Giovanni Falconi (stucco artist) and Tommaso Dolabella (painter). The most notable Polish artist of the era was Jerzy Siemiginowski-Eleuter, a court painter to King Jan III Sobieski. The Lwów-born artist is best remembered for four ornately painted ceilings depicting the seasons, created for the Wilanów Palace, Warsaw, in the 1680s. Portraiture also became highly popular in the Baroque era, and Daniel Schultz from Gdańsk was the most prominent

Altarpiece of St Mary's Basilica, Kraków

Of the Baroque art deposited in Poland by various Italian practitioners, Zygmunt's Column in Warsaw's Zamkowy Square is perhaps the most enduring. The figure (of Zygmunt III Waza) atop the column was sculpted by Clemente Molli in 1643. Over the centuries, the column has been restored on numerous occasions, most recently after the Nazis demolished it amid the 1944 Warsaw Uprising.

A dead likeness

The Sarmatian coffin portrait was a unique feature of Polish Baroque art. Polish nobles, who believed themselves descended from the ancient tribe of Sarmatian warriors, commissioned small, often hexagonal portraits painted on tin. The portrait was then placed on their coffin during elaborate funeral celebrations. The image was thought to represent the immortal soul of the deceased.

Polish exponent. His *Crimean Falconer of King John II Casimir with his Family* (1664) depicted Dedesh, the Crimean Agha who backed the Polish king in a war against the Russians.

Studying the Classics

As the opulence of Baroque gave way to the more sombre moods of Neoclassicism, the steady flow of foreign artists into Poland continued in the latter half of the 18th century. Italians such as Marcello Bacciarelli and, more significantly, Bernardo Bellotto (nephew of Canaletto), took prominence in the royal court. Bellotto's studied topographical paintings of Warsaw would later be used to help reconstruct the city after the Second World War. The most notable Polish artist of the period was Kazimierz Wojniakowski, a portraitist (and pupil of Bacciarelli) with a talent for clear Neoclassical lines and restrained colours. He painted the great and good of Polish society, notably *General Józef Kossakowski* (1794) and *Izabela Czartoryska* (1796).

General Józef Kossakowski

It took the loss of sovereignty for Poland to really discover its artistic identity. Inspired by Adam Mickiewicz and the other Romantic poets, Poland's 19th century painters made it their patriotic duty to preserve and promote a national character – something to which the emotive tendencies of Romanticism lent themselves well. They gathered in Kraków, then part of the Austrian Empire, where the occupiers' repression was less severe than in German- and Russian-controlled areas. The city's School of Drawing and Painting (later the Academy of Fine Arts (ASP)), founded in 1818, became a breeding ground for Polish talent. In particular, four 19th century painters became prominent and influential figures in the story of Polish art:

"Here, painter!"

As exclaimed by Pablo Picasso on discovering Piotr Michałowski's work in the National Museum in Warsaw.

Piotr Michałowski. Michałowski worked in various governmental posts in Kraków for a living and did his painting on the side, and yet he's one of the most expressive, acclaimed artists of the Romantic era. A period in exile in Paris helped develop his style, which majored on emotionally charged portraits, the subjects ranging from noble military commanders (fighting for the Polish cause) to humble peasants. However, he was perhaps most lauded for patriotic battle scenes of the Napoleonic wars, such as *Szarża w wąwozie Somosierra* (*The Charge at Somosierra*) (1837).

Artur Grottger. Grottger's short life (he died aged 30) was plagued by poor health and money troubles, but also enriched by the brooding battle scenes and landscapes of an accomplished Romantic painter. His most acclaimed works were cycles drawn in black and white chalk depicting the failed 1863 January Uprising. *Polonia* (1863), *Lithuania* (1865) and *Wojna* (*The War*) (1867) are all memorable.

Matejko's expensive muse

Jan Matejko married Teodora Giebułtowska in 1864. When she wasn't bearing the artist's children or posing for him, she loved to shop – Matejko's prolificacy as an artist is sometimes accredited to the need to pay off his wife's debts. In later life, Teodora suffered with mental health problems and she ended her days in an asylum.

Two more 19ᵗʰ century Polish patriotic painters

Józef Brandt. Painted rousing historical war scenes, such as *Bitwa pod Wiedniem* (*The Battle of Vienna*) (1873); most of them in exile.

Juliusz Kossak. Another expert at battle scenes, Kossak painted primarily in watercolour. *Odsiecz Smoleńska* (*The Relief of Smolensk*) (1882) depicted the Polish army taking on the Russians in the early 17th century.

Jan Matejko. A student, teacher and eventually president of the ASP (renamed the Akademia Sztuk Pięknych w Krakowie im. Jana Matejki (Jan Matejko Academy of Fine Arts) in 1979), Matejko painted some of the most iconic works of Polish art. He was another Romantic, painting huge, idealised scenes that showcased Poland's glorious past in an effort to stir the national spirit under occupation. Typically, he rendered battle scenes and key figures from national history, from Copernicus to Jan III Sobieski. Matejko's work brought him fame and no small fortune within his own lifetime.

Jan Matejko
(1838 – 1893)

Józef Chełmoński. A highly respected painter who favoured Realism over Romanticism, but who still sought to boost the identity of his homeland – not with battle scenes but with images of nature. In particular, he painted the landscape around Kuklówka Zarzeczna, the village in central Poland in which he settled after travelling widely through Europe. *Kuropatwy na śniegu* (*Partridge on the Snow*) (1891) and *Bociany* (*The Storks*) (1900) were typical.

Painting in code: Young Poland and the Symbolists
Towards the end of the 19th century, the Young Poland (Młoda Polska) movement (see section 1.2.3 for more) threw up a stylistically diverse bunch of artists. In common, like their Romantic forebears (and out of step with a prevailing Positivist current), they shared an emotionally charged version of patriotism, which they looked to convey through their work. However, their styles were more contemporary, employing the mysticism and dream imagery of Symbolism or the curvy lines of Art Nouveau to bring Polish art a modernity it had previously lacked. Three figures were particularly significant:

Matejko's *Bitwa pod Grunwaldem*

Writer Painter Polymath

Stanisław Wyspianski
(1869 – 1907)

Stanisław Wyspiański. A former student of Jan Matejko, Wyspiański was a man of many talents, being an influential poet and dramatist as well as a highly acclaimed painter. He worked predominantly in the Art Nouveau style, using pastels to create drawings such as *Autoportet* (*Self-portrait*) (1902) and *Macierzyństwo* (*Motherhood*) (1905), both featuring thick lines and floral motifs. Wyspiański is also remembered for his stained glass window designs, notably in the Franciscan Church in Kraków where he rendered the Creation on a grand scale in *Bóg Ojciec – Stań się* (*God the Father – Let it Be*) (1897-1904).

Jacek Malczewski. Another graduate of the Matejko ASP master class, Malczewski was Poland's most prominent Symbolist painter. His most famous work was *Melancholia* (1894), a painting rich with allegory and myth – it depicted the world on the brink of disaster, and made clear the connection with Poland's plight. Often, the artist painted his own portrait into his work.

Józef Mehoffer. Yet another student of Jan Matejko, Mehoffer collaborated with Stanisław Wyspiański on various decoration and stained glass projects, and was also well respected for his portraits of women, notably those of his wife Jadwiga. Mehoffer is also remembered for striking Symbolist paintings, in particular *Dziwny Ogród* (*Strange Garden*) (1903), ostensibly a sunny oil painting of his young son, his wife and the boy's nanny, but more likely a depiction of good (the boy) and bad (the large, nasty looking dragonfly in the painting's foreground).

Early movers of Polish design
When Stanisław Wyspiański retreated to the highland village of Zakopane he led other artists in the creation of a new aesthetic (see section 3.2.3 for more on the Zakopane style of architecture), named for the village and inspired by the folksy culture of the local Góral people. Wyspiański and others, notably Wojciech Brzega, gave Poland its first taste of organised (if highly derivative) interior design in the early 20th century; the Zakopane style majored on the use of carved wood, shaped in a rather rustic way. The Art Deco of the 1920s and 30s, the next big thing in Polish design, was infinitely slicker; the metalwork chandeliers and lamps of Henryk Grunwald and the furniture of Jan Kurzątkowski, including his *Piórka* (*Pens*) chair of 1930, highly modern.

Rytm method

The Rytm Association of Polish Artists was a 1920s collective that looked to combine Modernism with the more traditional tenets of painting – creating a link between past and present.

Zofia mans up for Munich

Zofia Stryjeńska posed as her brother to gain entry to the Munich Academy of Fine Arts in 1911 (at which time women weren't allowed to attend the college). She apparently kept the pretence up for an entire year.

Catching the Modernist mood

Poland's post-First World War independence went some way to freeing artists from the obligation of championing national identity. Instead, finally, they could explore and embrace the Modernist movements that were sweeping across Europe. The key genres that preoccupied Western art in the late 19th and early 20th centuries all had their Polish advocates:

The Formists

Contemporaneous with – and similar to – the Futurists of Italy, and introducing elements of Cubism into Poland, the avant-garde, theory-heavy Formists created a kind of Polish Expressionism in the years immediately after the First World War. Their most famous (although least typical) card-carrier was **Stanisław Ignacy Witkiewicz** (or just Witkacy – see section 4.2.3 for his work in theatre), who painted animalistic figures in dream-like landscapes, but the paintings of **Tymon Niesiołowski**, a significant Polish artist throughout the first half of the 20th century, were perhaps more emblematic of what the Formists were about – the subjects comprising 'forms' as much as figures.

Art Deco

The intense colours and geometric forms of Art Deco enjoyed their finest Polish hour in the hands of two female painters. Warsaw-born socialite **Tamara de Lempicka** was a portraitist, renowned for *Jeune Fille en Vert* (1927), a typically shadowy, gently blocky painting of a girl in a green dress, and *Autoportrait* (1925), an iconic self-portrait featuring a green Bugatti. **Zofia Stryjeńska** was perhaps the most famous Polish artist of the interwar period. Her paintings, often featuring colourful scenes of Slavic peoples in traditional dress, were inspired by native folklore, as seen in *Pory roku* (*The Four Seasons*) (1925), *Ogień* (*Fire*) (1928), and *Woda* (*Water*) (1928).

Stanisław Ignacy
Witkiewicz
'Witkacy'

(1885 – 1939)

Brush for hire

The multi-talented
Witkacy, son of the
equally talented
Stanisław Witkiewicz
(see section 3.2.3),
gave up on the Formists
in 1924 and instead
churned out hundreds of
portraits to commission.
The Stanisław Ignacy
Witkiewicz Portrait
Painting Firm set up
shop in Zakopane, the
Podhale village where
his father famously
developed an eponymous
style of architecture, and
offered customers five
basic forms of portrait.
The proceeds from the
company were split
between Witkacy's other
artistic endeavours and
the costs of his drug
habit.

Constructivism

A genre in which form and materials took priority over
subject matter, and which was pioneered in Poland
by **Henryk Stażewski**, an ex-Formist who graduated
to geometric abstraction with painting, relief work and
even interior design featuring blocky shapes and bold
lines; indeed, Stażewski founded Blok, a collective of
Constructivists and Cubists. Stażewski was inspired by

1. Identity: the
foundations
of Polish culture

2. Literature
and philosophy

**3. Art, architecture
and design**

4. Music, theatre,
and comedy

5. Cinema
and fashion

6. Media and
communications

7. Food and drink

8. Living culture:
the state of
modern Poland

Nikifor the naïve
One of the most original Polish artists of the interwar period was Nikifor, a self-taught painter whose unintentionally childlike art, documenting the towns and countryside encountered in his itinerant life, was praised by the artistic elite for its simplicity and sincerity. Today, his paintings are collected as fine examples of naïve art. Posterity records that Nikifor's real name was Epifan Drowniak, but other details about the artist are less clear: different sources record him variously as an illiterate beggar and the son of a deaf mute prostitute who called himself Nikifor because he couldn't remember his real name.

another pioneer of the avant-garde in Poland, **Władysław Strzemiński**, who formulated Unism, the idea that a work of art stood alone – that a painting was defined by itself, an image in a frame, separate from its surrounds. On the canvas, his theory emerged in work that varied from clean geometric shapes (which also transferred to furniture design) to multiple wiggly lines. Strzemiński's wife, sculptor **Katarzyna Kobro**, was part of the Constructivist clique, creating geometric work such as *Konstrukcje wiszące 2* (*Hanging Construction 2*) (1921), an arrangement of simple steel ribbons and shapes.

Cubism

The reconstructed geometry of Cubism found its prime Polish advocate in Tadeusz Makowski. However, his was a relatively soft (and short-lived) Cubism, keen to mix the cones and cylinders pioneered by his friend Picasso with the brushstrokes of the post-Impressionists. His most avant-garde work featured figures, notably in *Trzej grajkowie* (*Three Musicians*) (1928) and *Jazz* (1929), but he was also popular for a series of more conventional rural landscapes.

Colourful clique: the Kapists
The small brushstrokes of post-Impressionism, jabbed colourfully onto the canvas to capture movement and light, informed the Polish Colourists who came together in the 1920s and did much to shape the country's art over the subsequent two decades. Hanging around in Paris soaking up the vibes, the group called itself the Paris Committee (Komitet Paryski) – and became known as the Kapists. Where predecessors had used art as a call to arms, they focussed instead on the aesthetic qualities of their painting. **Józef Pankiewicz** was the major representative, known for accomplished – if somewhat

unadventurous – landscapes including *Pejzaź południowy z domem* (*Southern Landscape with a House*) (c.1925) and *Pejzaź z Cassis* (*Cassis Landscape*) (1928). Jan Cybis, Eugeniusz Geppert and Józef Czapski were also important amongst the Kapists.

Socialist Realism adds a gloss finish

The adoption of Socialist Realism (see section 1.2.3) as blanket cultural policy by the post-war Communist government inevitably stifled the visual arts. It was peddled as the truthful representation of reality but was more like 'Socialist Romanticism', with the common man portrayed as a heroic figure in a glorious Stalinist future. The paintings and sculpture that emerged were, however well executed, unsurprisingly staid. Aleksander Kobzdej's homage to Polish builders, *Podaj cegłę* (*Pass the Brick*) (1950), was typical – its subjects constructing their wall with quiet determination.

Poster boys of Polish art

Poster design occupies a well-respected niche in the story of 20th century Polish art (it even has its own museum, founded in Wilanów, Warsaw, in 1968). It began with tourism and general advertising posters, and artists like Stefan Norblin and Tadeusz Gronowski in the 1920s and 30s. Their work was characterised by an artistic excellence rarely associated with such ephemeral media. This quality continued into the Soviet era, during which accomplished artists like Włodzimierz Zakrzewski produced finely honed propaganda (of noble miners and heroic soldiers) for the authorities. In the 1950s and '60s, Polish poster art enjoyed a golden age, realised in particular in the film poster: Henryk Tomaszewski, Eryk Lipiński and Wiktor Górka all designed stunning posters for Film Polski, the state distribution company. Because the posters weren't considered 'serious' art, they didn't always suffer the state scrutiny enforced on other visual art forms, and artists duly enjoyed some degree of expression, layering the posters with oblique messages that had little to do with the film in question.

In the climate of tight state control, Andrzej Wróblewski stood out. At the Kraków Academy of Fine Arts, Wróblewski rebelled against the prevailing taste for Colourism and created his own disturbing, Surrealist style using stark blues and greens. His best-known series of paintings, *Rozstrzelania* (*Executions*), featured dismembered bodies, placed amid the brutality of Nazi occupation. The likes of *Rozstrzelanie z chłopczykiem* (*Execution of a Boy*) (1949) and *Rozstrzelanie na ścianie* (*Execution Against a Wall*) (1949) were shocking. Wróblewski went on to produce some unremarkable works in the Socialist Realism style in the early 1950s before dying in a climbing accident, aged 29.

Relaxing the rules (slightly)

When Stalin died, the Polish authorities gained more control over cultural policy. They relaxed the rules somewhat and gave artists more freedom, allowing for greater expression and increased access to new ideas and trends (specifically those from the West). A handful of noteworthy artists from the post-Stalinist years have lived on in the collective memory:

Tadeusz Kantor. An artist who became renowned for his work in avant-garde set design and theatre direction (see section 4.2.4 for more), but who was also a key figure in Poland's post-war visual arts scene. He went from dark, simplified figures in the immediate post-war period to canvases filled with spots and lines of paint, daubed in vibrant colour, in the mid 1950s. He described them as 'secretions of his inner self'.

Alina Szapocznikow. A sculptor whose provocative work in the 1960s and '70s turned polyester casts of her lips and breasts into everyday objects like lamps – *Usta iluminowane I* (*Lips Illuminated I*) (1966) – and vases – *Deser III* (*Dessert III*) (1971). Szapocznikow's work is increasingly sought after today.

Władysław Hasior. Another sculptor, Hasior found international recognition with both gallery work and outdoor installations made from old prams, chairs, wheels, broken toys and other *objets trouvés*. *Czarny krajobraz I – Dzieciom Zamojszczyzny* (*Black Landscape I – to the Children of Zamojszczyzna*) (1974) featured a child's pram filled with soil, candles and crucifixes, whilst *Ogniste ptaki* (*Fire Birds*) (1975) made recycled metal into bird shapes.

Magdalena Abakanowicz. Abakanowicz came to international prominence in the 1960s with pioneering sculptures known as Abakans, which, woven from old harbour ropes and suspended from the ceiling, seemed to defy categorisation. Since the 1980s, Abakanowicz has produced monumental humanoid figures in metals, often placed in large groups and usually without heads or arms. They represent the modern world's crisis of identity. *Puellae* (1992) featured 30 headless bronze figures placed in the sculpture garden of the National Gallery of Art in Washington DC.

A golden age for Polish design
The 1950s and 60s in Poland produced some outstanding design work, much of which has now become highly sought after. The Alfa 35mm camera (1958), Osa scooter (1959) and Bambino gramophone (1967) are all deemed classics today. The period also produced experimental furniture, such as the plywood *Muszelka* (*Shell*) chair (1956) by Teresa Kruszewska, and Roman Modzelewski's blobby fibreglass armchair of 1958. Unfortunately, a lack of funding and the limitations of Polish industry meant that such designs were never mass-produced. Indeed, from the 1960s onwards, the vast majority of Poles had to be content with cheap modular furniture, the most ubiquitous being Bogusława and Czesław Kowalski's chipboard wall units, 'System MK'.

1. Identity: the   2. Literature   **3. Art, architecture**   4. Music, theatre,   5. Cinema   6. Media and   7. Food and drink   8. Living culture:
foundations   and philosophy   **and design**   and comedy   and fashion   communications   the state of
of Polish culture   modern Poland

In search of a cause: art in contemporary Poland

In the years since Poland voted out the Communists, the country has nurtured a good crop of young artists; practitioners who are respected at home and abroad, and who address the multiplicity of issues – social, sexual, religious, political and historical (the Holocaust in particular) – affecting modern Poles. What has changed, perhaps, is Polish art's long-held enthusiasm for addressing and celebrating national identity – today, the themes are more universal.

Five contemporary artists

Artur Żmijewski. A prolific video artist, Żmijewski's challenging work addresses the socio-political issues of the day. For *Ja i AIDS* (*Me and AIDS*) (1996) he created a film that showed three terrified naked people – two men and one woman – running into each other at full speed. And in *Berek* (*The Game of Tag*) (1999) he filmed naked men and women playing tag in a former concentration camp gas chamber.

Mirosław Bałka. Bałka's intensely personal and often confusing sculpture and paintings have made use of everyday materials as diverse and unlikely as soap, human hair, ash and rust. His most famous piece to date is *How It Is* (*2009*), a sculpture/ installation redolent of the Holocaust, first displayed in Tate Modern's turbine hall, London. The work features a giant steel container – 30 metres long, 13 metres high and set on two-metre-high stilts – with a pitch black interior inside which the viewer can walk round.

Mirosław Bałka's fountain

Katarzyna Kozyra. A sculptor and video artist who came to public attention with the controversial *Piramida* zwierząt (*Animal Pyramid*) (1993), a sculpture with four stuffed animals – a cockerel, a cat, a dog and a horse – standing one on top of the other. The work included a film showing the killing of the horse, which the artist carried out herself. Other acclaimed works include *Święto wiosny* (*The Rite of Spring*) (1999-2002), a video installation featuring stop-frame animation of aging, naked figures convulsing on a white background.

Joanna Rajkowska. Rajkowska's *Pozdrowienia z Alej Jerozolimskich* (*Greetings from Jerusalem Avenue*) (2002) was a 15-metre tall artificial palm tree installed in Jerusalem Avenue in Warsaw. She hoped the work would draw attention to the name of the street and to the role Jews have played in Polish history. The work was only supposed to stay in place for a year, but it remains, and has become a much-visited landmark.

Paweł Althamer. A video and installation artist known best for *One of Many* (2007), an exhibition celebrating the human body, in which his own figure was reproduced in various different forms, not least as a 20-metre long inflatable naked doll.

Bags, stools and sofas: contemporary design
Poland's burgeoning market economy supports a growing number of young designers, each carving a reputation with innovative work both at home and abroad. Tomek Rygalik is one such figure, the winner of numerous awards and known for furniture like the *Tennis* armchair (2008), its design interlocking a bit (and only a bit) like a tennis ball. Another, Oskar Zięta, impressed with the *Plopp* stool (2007), constructed of thin, inflated steel sheets, whilst Agata Kulik and Paweł Pomorski (working under the auspices of MALAFOR) have created the *Trunks* stool (2005), hewn from tree trunks and steel, and *Blow* (2010), a sofa made from inflated paper bags. Finally, Katarzyna Okińczyc and Remigiusz Truchanowicz have enjoyed collaborative success, designing the *60 Bag* (2008), an environmentally friendly bag that takes about two months to completely biodegrade.

"I FEEL LIKE A COSMONAUT IN THE SUIT OF MY OWN BODY. I AM A TRAPPED SOUL. THE BODY PLAYS A ROLE OF A DRESS, OF AN ADDRESS. MY BODILY ADDRESS IS PAWEŁ ALTHAMER"
Paweł Althamer

3.2 Architecture

Considering the destruction brought by various wars, Poland's rich architectural heritage survives in reasonable condition. The structural landscape pitches thousand-year-old stone churches alongside stern Soviet-era blocks and shiny modern skyscrapers.

1. Identity: the foundations of Polish culture

2. Literature and philosophy

3. Art, architecture and design

4. Music, theatre, and comedy

5. Cinema and fashion

6. Media and communications

7. Food and drink

8. Living culture: the state of modern Poland

St Leonard's Crypt, Wawel Castle, Kraków (c.1040). Built by Casimir I the Restorer in the 11th century and now the resting place of various Polish kings and heroes.

St Prokop's Church

St Prokop's Church, Strzelno (12th century). With a nave shaped like a Roman rotunda.

St Andrew's Church, Kraków (late 11th century). A church built with defence in mind, as evidenced by monumental walls and tiny windows.

Ancient inspiration: Poland does Romanesque

Poland, like much of Europe, soaked up the Romanesque style of architecture in the late Middle Ages. It came to the country with the Piast's conversion to Christianity (see section 1.2.1), brought by foreign clerics who built churches and monasteries inspired by a mix of Roman form and Byzantine style. Typically, Poland's Romanesque buildings had very thick walls and chunky piers in support of barrel vaults and high rounded arches. Limited light found its way in through high clerestory windows. Only 100 or so Polish Romanesque buildings have survived through to the modern era, and many of these have experienced alteration in the intervening centuries. A handful, such as the Collegiate Church of St Mary and St Alexius at Tum, have retained their stone carvings.

Towering Gothic

The wealth of Poland's clergy blessed the country with hundreds of elegant new buildings during the Gothic explosion of the 13th century. Again, the craftsmen and architects were brought in by foreign Christian orders. Where Romanesque had been chunky and dark, Gothic employed progressive building techniques – ribbed vaults and flying buttresses allowed for thinner walls and larger

windows – to create tall, light-filled monuments to the fervour of Polish faith. Arches became pointed and the stone tracery increasingly elaborate. Gothic would live on longer in Poland than elsewhere, remaining important to religious architecture for a good 300 years.

St Andrew's Church, Kraków

94

The Gothic era also gifted numerous secular buildings to Poland. Markets, town halls and even entire towns were built in the Gothic style – Kazimierz, the historic Jewish quarter of Kraków was founded as a 'new town' by Kazimierz the Great in 1335 and became a tightly knit network of Gothic houses and synagogues, almost all of which was destroyed in the Second World War. The same ruler also commissioned a raft of castles in the south of the country, such as Będzin, a giant in grey stone, built with two chunky towers, one cylindrical, the other square. In northern Poland, the Teutonic Knights built their own collection of fortified castles, outshining Kazimierz' stout, functional builds with more elaborate, Hanseatic-style turreted buildings in red brick.

Three of the best Gothic buildings in Poland

Wrocław Town Hall (begun c.1300). Built and adapted over three centuries, Wrocław's *Ratusz* features elaborate stone tracery.

St Mary's Basilica, Kraków (14th century). Built in brick, Kraków's biggest church has 80-metre-high asymmetrical towers.

Malbork Castle (completed 1406). The finest of the Teutonic Knights' fortresses, now a UNESCO World Heritage Site, is the largest castle in the world, covering 143,591 square metres.

Castles in the air

Poland is blessed with several medieval castles, including a number known as the 'Eagles' Nests', built high up on rocky outcrops in the 14th century by Kazimierz the Great. The Eagles' Nests Trail in the south-west of the country has become popular with energetic tourists, taking in 25 castles along its 163 km route.

3.2.2 Degrees of Classicism: Renaissance, Baroque and Neoclassical architecture

Italian by design: the early Renaissance

In the Renaissance, the patronage of Polish architecture transferred from the Church to the royal court and the nobility. The first half of the 16th century witnessed an influx of Italian architects and craftsmen, invited to Poland by the great and

Wawel Castle, Kraków

the good to create buildings of wealth and status. King Zygmunt the Old led the way, employing Bartolommeo Berrecci to transform Kraków's Gothic royal castle at Wawel into a spectacular Renaissance palace. Symmetry ruled, with slim columns and pilasters, semicircular arches and arcaded courtyards. The Polish nobles followed Zygmunt's lead, using foreign expertise to transform their castles into palaces.

Mannerism stretches out the Renaissance

In the later 16th century, Renaissance architecture spread through Poland's towns and cities and, influenced by new trends emergent in Italy, the Netherlands, Hungary and Germany, began displaying elements of Mannerism. Reacting against the restrained Classical symmetry of the early Renaissance, Mannerism introduced uneven proportions and extravagant loggias, arcaded courtyards and side towers. The nobles remained obsessed with their castles, building new quadrilateral fortresses gathered around an enclosed courtyard. Baranów Sandomerski Castle, built between 1591-1606 in the south-east of the country, was typical, its Mannerist style emerging in curved staircases, bell-shaped turrets and a lavishly decorated roofline.

Decoration overload: Baroque

The Mannerism of the late Renaissance prevailed in Poland well into the 17th century, notably at Kalwaria Zebrzydowska, a site of pilgrimage comprising a church and several chapels inspired by the medieval layout of Jerusalem. Eventually, however, the lavish styling of Baroque began to infiltrate architecture. Baroque buildings were characterised by grandeur and complexity; they made use of bright colours, ornate decoration, domes and multiple windows – imbuing the Classicism of the Renaissance with a heightened frippery. The nobility and the Church, re-empowered by the Counter Reformation, used Baroque buildings to declaim their power and wealth. The Italian-designed Church of St Peter and St Paul in Kraków (1619) was an early example, funded by King Zygmunt III Waza for the Jesuit order and featuring the kind of curvy façade typical of the Baroque era (the interior was less impressive, the builders having blown the budget on the façade). At Wilanów Palace, near Warsaw, Polish Baroque hit a high note with a lavish royal residence, built for King Jan Sobieski by Italian architect Agostino Locci between 1677 and 1696.

Zamoyski goes out on a limb

Zamość, in south-east Poland, was founded in 1580, conceived by the powerful statesman Jan Zamoyski as the ideal fortified Renaissance town. The layout, designed by Italian architect Bernardo Morando, was based on the human form: the palace represented the head, the main streets the spine and arms, fortified bastions the hands and legs and the squares internal organs. Zamość's heart lay in the Great Market Square surrounded by arcaded houses. In 1992 the town centre was granted UNESCO World Heritage Site status.

Wilanów Palace

1. Identity: the
foundations
of Polish culture

2. Literature
and philosophy

**3. Art, architecture
and design**

4. Music, theatre,
and comedy

5. Cinema
and fashion

6. Media and
communications

7. Food and drink

8. Living culture:
the state of
modern Poland

Baroque buildings in Poland (as elsewhere) were often highly ostentatious, none more so than Krzyżtopór Palace, built within five-sided fortifications in Ujazd, a village in the south of the country. Named for its owner, Krzysztof Ossoliński, the palace was constructed between 1627 and 1644. The building boasted four towers (one for each season), 12 ballrooms (for the months), 52 rooms (for each week of the year) and 365 windows (you know why). A ceiling in the main reception room was made of crystal and served as an aquarium stocked with exotic fish. Alas, the palace has been in ruins since the Russians attacked in the 18th century, and to date no one has been able to afford the required restoration work.

Return to form: Neoclassicism

The rampaging ostentation of Baroque brought a backlash in the later years of the 18th century. Neoclassical architecture reined in the flamboyance with its simple balance and symmetry. Tall columns and subdued Palladian porticos became de rigueur and the Renaissance connection with Antiquity was renewed. It was also a period in which Poland finally nurtured a good crop of homegrown architects, figures like Christian Piotr Aigner, designer of the colonnaded Temple of the Sibyl in Puławy (1797), Wawrzyniec Gucewicz (Vilnius Town Hall (1799)) and Stanisław Zawadzki (Skórzewski Palace, Lubostroń (1800)). Meanwhile, Italian-born architect-to-the-royals, Dominik Merlini, designed two of Poland's most lauded Neoclassical builds – Jabłonna Palace (1779) and Łazienki Palace (1764-95), the latter built in Warsaw's Royal Baths Park and duly known as the Palace on the Water.

Jabłona Palace

3.2.3 Wood, concrete and steel:
modern Polish architecture

Building up the past: revivalism

In the dark years of Partition, Polish architecture sought out symbolic expressions of national identity by creating buildings that harked back to the country's days of power and freedom. Romanesque, Renaissance and Baroque styles were all revisited but neo-Gothic architecture proved most popular, adjudged more 'Polish' than the other schools. Countless public, private and sacred buildings were constructed or remodelled in the Gothic style. The Chapel of Blessed Bronisława (1861), designed

Chapel of Blessed Bronisław, Kraków

by Feliks Księżarski, was a strange mix of pointy arches and crenulations built at the foot of Kraków's Kościuszko mound, whilst Jan Pius Dziekoński's Cathedral of the Virgin Mary (1899-1908), in Radom, had delicate stonework, ribbed vaulting and a rose window as per the Gothic of old – and the towers took inspiration from St Mary's Basilica in Kraków (see section 3.2.1).

Back to basics: Zakopane

The most successful attempt to cultivate a national brand of architecture unfurled in Zakopane, the mountain village that lent its name to the attendant building style. The driving force was Stanisław Witkiewicz, the art critic, architect and painter who, frustrated by the Swiss-style chalets being built in the highlands of the Podhale region in the late 19th century, attempted instead to create indigenous buildings constructed using the centuries-old traditions of the area. He hoped to create a house that would 'possess the full range of comforts yet simultaneously be beautiful in a fundamentally Polish way'. The initial result was Zakopane's Villa Koliba (1892-94), which successfully echoed the traditional wooden buildings and furnishing styles of the Carpathian Mountains, threw in some elements of Art Nouveau, and which would serve as a great inspiration in this region and beyond for years to come.

99

Built to last

The Art Deco Prudential building was hit by more than 1,000 shells in the Warsaw Uprising of 1944. Where older, surrounding buildings crumbled, the tower block was saved by its steel frame. Briefly, during the battle, the Polish resistance managed to fly their flag from the TV antenna on the structure's roof. The Prudential was saved during the Soviet era, but gained an inappropriate Neoclassical colonnade in the process; work is now underway to remove these embellishments, returning the Prudential to its Art Deco glory.

The brief Modernist flourish

Poland's newfound independence coincided with an influx of new ideas in the late 19th and early 20th centuries. Art Nouveau made a limited impact, its main movers confining their activity to the city of Łódź, before Modernism arrived and architects broke with classical tradition, taking their lead instead from functionalism and simplicity. The availability of new materials, namely concrete and steel, provided the opportunity to put new styles into practice. This growth spurt reached a peak in the interwar years, when Polish cities were stocked with the sleek curves of Art Deco and straight lines of the International Style. Alas, very little of it survived the Second World War.

The Prudential Building, Warsaw, during and after the war

1. Identity: the foundations of Polish culture
2. Literature and philosophy
3. Art, architecture and design
4. Music, theatre, and comedy
5. Cinema and fashion
6. Media and communications
7. Food and drink
8. Living culture: the state of modern Poland

Centennial Hall (1911-13). A monumental reinforced concrete cupola measuring 69 metres wide and 42 metres high, built by Max Berg in Wrocław when the city was still part of Germany.

Drapacz Chmur (1929-34). Poland's first skyscraper (or *drapacz chmur*) was built with a steel frame to a height of 60 metres in Katowice by Tadeusz Kozłowski.

Prudential (1931-34). A fine, simple Art Deco tower designed by Marcin Weinfeld and erected as the Polish home of the Prudential Insurance Company in Świętokrzyska Street, Warsaw.

Zalewski's Villa (1931). Designed by Bohdan Pniewski and built in the Saska Kępa district of Warsaw, the cuboid, flat-roofed villa was about as close as Poland got to the functionalism of Swiss architect Le Corbusier.

St Roch Church (1927-46). Oskar Sosnowski's blocky Białystok church is an octahedron with an 83-metre-tall tower.

Bloc party: the buildings of Socialist Realism

The Second World War ravaged the historic architecture of Polish towns and cities. Bomb damage was extensive – in Warsaw, for example, 85 per cent of pre-war buildings were destroyed, including the Royal Castle, which would endure years of painstaking reconstruction after being dynamited by the Nazis in the Uprising of 1944. After the war, the new Soviet-controlled government dictated architectural style in the same way that it did all other forms of culture. In the Stalinist era, building design fell within the confines of Socialist Realism (see section 1.2.3), which brought a thick weight to the lines of Modernism and blended it with Classical motifs. New civic structures were to be monumental, built in concrete and lightly adorned with columns and statues of heroic workers.

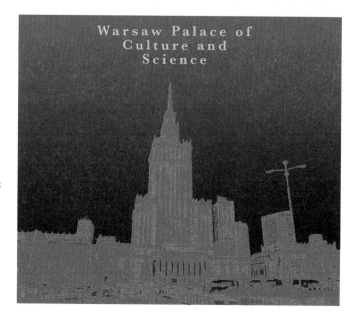
Warsaw Palace of Culture and Science

The elephant in the room (is wearing lacy underwear)

The residents of Warsaw have given the Palace of Science and Culture various derogatory names over the years, including *słoń w koronkowych gatkach* (the elephant in lacy underwear). When the Communist regime left power in 1989, a debate ensued about whether or not to pull the building down.

The architectural showpiece of Socialist Realism was Warsaw's Palace of Culture and Science. At 231 metres high it was (and still is) the tallest building in the country, its central block topped by a soaring spire and cornered by four identical feet. The Neoclassical adornments, including sculptures of Adam Mickiewicz and Nikolaus Copernicus, were supposed to evoke Polishness, but to the Poles the building was inherently imperial. Designed by Russian Lev Rudnev (who visited the United States to learn about skyscraper construction), and built between 1952 and 1955, it was framed as a gift to the Polish people from the Soviet Union. Most, however, viewed the palace as a statement of Stalin's dominion over Poland and its citizens. Other Socialist Realist projects in the 1950s were less declamatory but similarly imposing. Huge housing districts were built in Warsaw and Wrocław, the Marszałkowska Dzielnica Mieszkaniowa (MDM) and Kościuszkowa Dzielnica Mieszkaniowa (KDM) respectively; and the new town of Nowa Huta, a centre of heavy industry populated by the workers, was established next door to 'bourgeois' Kraków.

102

1. Identity: the foundations of Polish culture   2. Literature and philosophy   **3. Art, architecture and design**   4. Music, theatre, and comedy   5. Cinema and fashion   6. Media and communications   7. Food and drink   8. Living culture: the state of modern Poland

Utility reigns

Expediency soon overtook the statement building of the 1950s. In the 1960s and '70s, Polish architecture was governed by housing shortages and a lack of funding. Most building took the form of soulless *wielka płyta*, residential blocks (aka *bloki*), poorly designed and poorly built, made from large prefabricated concrete panels. Such developments still blight the Polish landscape. The occasional pieces of genuine architecture that did make it off the drawing board moved away from Neoclassicism towards a purity of form led by straight lines and a 'space age' form of Modernism. The saucer-shaped Spodek arena (1971) in Katowice, designed by Maciej Gintowt and Maciej Krasiński, and Nowa Huta's Arka Pana church (1977), reminiscent of an arc, designed by Wojciech Pietrzyk and Jan Grabacki, are two examples.

Building boom: contemporary architecture

To most modern Poles, the general public at least, the stark buildings of the Communist era remain hugely unfashionable, hated even. And yet, a raft of young architects fight to conserve and convert these structures from the 1960s and '70s into new public spaces, arguing that each represents a very Polish response to the confines of life under Soviet rule and should be preserved as such.

Today, new buildings proliferate in Poland, thanks to the private, public and EU investment that has helped resurrect the country since the fall of the Communist regime. Much of the new architecture has taken the form of uninspiring shopping malls and skyscrapers, built in glass and steel in a style recognised around the Western world. However, investment has also attracted world-renowned architects to work on showcase projects, such as Norman Foster's Metropolitan (2003)

Wavy blocks

Thousands of urban Poles still live in the ugly concrete *bloki mieszkalne* (residential blocks) or simply *bloki* of the Communist era. The most intriguing variant is the *falowiec*, meaning 'wavy block', a very long building constructed in a zigzag fashion in the 1970s. Gdansk has eight *falowiec*; the best known is in Obronców Wybrzeża Street; it's 11 storeys high, stretches 860 metres in length and requires three separate bus stops along the way for its 7,000 residents.

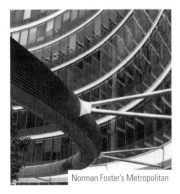

Norman Foster's Metropolitan

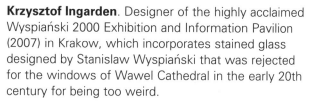

Złota 44

Bending the blueprints

Krzywy Domek (Crooked House) (2004) in Sopot is thought to be Poland's most photographed building. Designed by Szotynscy Zaleski, the three-storey construction would blend nicely with its neighbours in the Rezident shopping centre were it not for its distorted dimensions; squashed and curved, the building looks like it is being reflected in a fairground mirror.

office building in Warsaw, and the Złota 44 residential skyscraper in Warsaw (2012), designed by Daniel Libeskind, a Polish-born architect who has taken up US citizenship. Equally, a progressive group of homegrown architects have emerged to take Polish architecture forward.

Five important contemporary architecture practices

Stefan Kuryłowicz. The creative force behind the cube-like Focus Filtrowa office building (2001) and the Prosta Tower (2010), with its distinctive concrete latticework façade; both have helped define Warsaw's post-Communist skyline. Kuryłowicz died in a plane crash in 2011.

Krzysztof Ingarden. Designer of the highly acclaimed Wyspiański 2000 Exhibition and Information Pavilion (2007) in Krakow, which incorporates stained glass designed by Stanislaw Wyspiański that was rejected for the windows of Wawel Cathedral in the early 20th century for being too weird.

Robert Konieczny. Known in particular for *Dom Bezpieczny* (*Safe House*) (2009), on the outskirts of Warsaw, built with movable parts that enable the building to fold in on itself forming a solid grey block.

Jan Kubec and Magdalena Gilner. Collectively RAr-2 Laboratorium Architektury, designers of the acclaimed Copernicus Science Centre (Centrum Nauki Kopernik) (2010) overlooking the Vistula in Warsaw, which houses exhibition spaces, laboratories and a planetarium.

**Natalia Paszkowska, Marcin Mostafa,
and Wojciech Kakowski.**
Part of the WWAA collective that designed the Polish
Pavilion for the Shanghai Expo 2010, creating a building
clad in perforated material, inspired by the paper cut-outs
of Polish folk art.

Plan and
reality:
Poland's
beautiful
pavilion for
Expo 2010 in
Shanghai

1. Identity: the
foundations
of Polish culture

2. Literature
and philosophy

**3. Art, architecture
and design**

4. Music, theatre,
and comedy

5. Cinema
and fashion

6. Media and
communications

7. Food and drink

8. Living culture:
the state of
modern Poland

4 Music, theatre and comedy

4.1 Music

From the folk melodies of Chopin to the protest punk of Brygada Kryzys, music has been used to bolster and celebrate Polish identity for centuries. The result is a rich, intelligent repertoire with a special resonance to Polish ears.

4.1.1 In the shadow of Chopin: classical music

If you only ever listen to five pieces of Polish classical music...

Piano Concerto No. 1 in E minor, Op. 11 (1830) by Fryderyk Chopin.

Piano Quintet in G minor, Op. 34 (1885) by Juliusz Zarębski.

Symphony No. 4, Op. 60 (1932) by Karol Szymanowski.

Symphony No. 3, Op. 36 'Symphony of Sorrowful Songs' (1977) by Henryk Górecki.

Violin Concerto No. 2 'Metamorphoses' (1995) by Krzysztof Penderecki.

To most people, many Poles included, Polish classical music means one thing: Fryderyk Chopin. However, even though his legacy dominates, and there are numerous events dedicated to his works – notably the Chopin festivals in Duszniki-Zdrój and Warsaw – Poland has actually produced several esteemed composers over the centuries.

Music goes super-phonic

Classical music arrived in Poland with Christianity in the 11th century, carried along on the monophonic (single melodic line) Gregorian chant of medieval monks. The earliest nameable composer was Wincenty z Kielczy, a Dominican friar who wrote the famous *Gaude mater Polonia* (c. 1253), a hymn still used today on certain official occasions. Gradually, as polyphony (having two or more melodic lines) appeared, music became more sophisticated. Poland's earliest surviving polyphonic work is *Omnia beneficia*, a piece for four voices that dates from the first half of the 14th century but which was lost until 1970 when it surfaced at a convent in Stary Sącz, southern Poland. The foremost medieval Polish polyphonic composer was Mikołaj z Radomia, remembered in particular for two motets: *Hystorigraphi aciem mentis* and *Magnificat* (both mid 15th century).

Golden age greats

Music flourished in the 16th century 'Golden Age' of the Renaissance, led by new instruments, such as the violins of the great Marcin Groblicz and Baltazar Dankwart, and advances in musicianship and composition. Foreign (particularly Italian) influences played their part in Kraków's royal court, where Zygmunt I Stary and Zygmunt II August gave generous patronage to the era's two key composers:

Mikołaj Gomółka. His only known work was the monumental *Melodie na psałterz polski* (1580), with all 150 Psalms set to simple, elegant music designed for amateurs to play at home.

Wacław z Szamotuł. Amongst the greatest of all Renaissance composers, Szamotuł's works include the motet *In te, Domine, speravi* (1554) and his best known, the sacred song *Modlitwa, gdy dziatki spać idą* (c.1550).

Ornate sounds of the Baroque

The foreign influences grew in the 17th century, led by the Italian musicians who would come to outnumber their Polish counterparts at the new royal court in Warsaw. Most of the music of the period was Baroque in style, characterised by complex and ornate compositions. Two Polish contributors stood out:

Mikołaj Zieleński. The masterly composer of polychoral music, best remembered for the sizeable *Offertoria totius anni* and *Communiones totius anni* (both published 1611), which contained over 100 sacred pieces for use during the liturgical year.

Adam Jarzębski. A violinist at the royal court, known for excellent concertos and other instrumental works, as found in *Canzoni e Concerti* (1627).

Slowly does it: high times for the polonaise

Music fell in step with the wider cultural quest for national identity during Poland's Enlightenment, drawing on the melodies and rhythms of traditional folk styles. The polonaise, originally a slow folk dance with musical accompaniment in triple time (having three beats to the bar), became hugely popular in polite society, and almost every composer in the country wrote their own interpretation. Three in particular drew heavily on the country's folk traditions:

Michał Ogiński. A diplomat and composer who wrote mazurkas (a faster folk dance from Mazovia) as well as many polonaises, most notably the famous *Pożegnanie ojczyzny* (1794).

Maria Szymanowska. A pianist whose compositions included polonaises and mazurkas, although she is best known as a virtuoso performer.

Józef Elsner. A prolific exponent of the polonaise, but nevertheless best remembered for an impressive oratorio, *Passio Domini Nostri Jesu Christi* (1837), and for being the teacher of Fryderyk Chopin, the greatest writer of the polonaise.

The age of Chopin

Fryderyk Chopin is considered Poland's greatest composer. Every Pole, young or old, has heard one or two of his works at the very least. He put Poland on the map in what was a desperate time for the country, making use of the native folk melodies and dances – the polonaise, mazurka and krakowiak – to stir national pride. Born in Żelazowa Wola, central Poland, to a French emigré father and Polish mother, he was a child prodigy, writing his first polonaise as a seven year old and giving his first public performances a year later. Having completed his musical studies in Warsaw, Chopin travelled the European capitals, drawing acclaim with the breathtaking virtuosity of his piano playing and composition.

Jósef

Two for one: the mazurka
In Polish the word *mazurek* refers to a stylised (classical) dance/composition based on an old folk dance such as a *mazur*, *kujaiwak* or *oberek* (see section 4.1.2 for all three), as immortalised by Chopin. Confusingly, two different words, *mazur* (the folk dance) and *mazurek* (the stylised classical composition) both translate into English as 'mazurka'.

Naming the polonaise
'Polonaise' is the feminine French word for 'Polish', itself drawn from the Latin name for Poland, 'Polonia'.

"THE THREE MOST CELEBRATED DOCTORS ON THE ISLAND HAVE BEEN TO SEE ME. THE FIRST SAID I WAS DEAD, THE SECOND THAT I WAS DYING AND THE THIRD THAT I AM GOING TO DIE."
Fryderyk Chopin, feeling off-colour in Majorca in 1838 – he lived for another 11 years.

Frédéric Chopin
(1810 – 1849)

Three famous works by Chopin

Waltz in D flat major, Op. 64, No. 1 (1847). Popularly known as the *Minute Waltz*, even though it takes about two minutes to play.

Piano Sonata No. 2, Op. 35 (1839). Includes, in the third movement, the well-known 'der, der, der-der' of the *Funeral March* (played at Chopin's own funeral).

Polonaise in A major, Op. 40, No. 1 (1838). Commonly known as the *Military Polonaise*, the piece was broadcast daily on national radio during the German invasion of Poland in 1939.

Two more greats from the Romantic period

Henryk Wieniawski. A renowned violin player whose best compositions included *Violin Concerto No. 1, Op. 14* (1853).

Juliusz Zarębski. A student of Franz Liszt and virtuoso pianist, who, in addition to polonaises and mazurkas, wrote the sublime *Piano Quintet in G minor, Op. 34* (1885) before his death from tuberculosis aged 31.

Living outside Poland in adult life, Chopin remained a staunch patriot, deeply concerned and affected by his country's plight. He apparently wrote *Étude Op. 10, No. 12* (1831), the famous piano solo known as the *Revolutionary Étude*, to express his anguish at the 1830 November Uprising. French author George Sand (pseudonym of Amandine-Aurore Lucille Dupin, Baronne Dudevant), with whom he had a stormy ten-year relationship, described him as 'more Polish than Poland'. His music, characterised by a melodic subtlety and dynamic range, and written largely for solo piano, included preludes, waltzes, nocturnes, mazurkas and polonaises. Blighted throughout his life by ill health, probably tuberculosis, Chopin died aged 39 in Paris having never returned to his homeland.

Home is where the heart is

Fryderyk Chopin's dying wish was for his heart to be removed before his funeral at Père Lachaise cemetery in Paris in 1849. There were two reasons for this: firstly to satisfy his taphophobia, which, as everyone knows, is the fear of being buried alive; and secondly so that his elder sister, Ludwika, could smuggle his heart, preserved in cognac, back to Poland. While Chopin's body remains in France, his heart now rests in a crystal urn at Warsaw's Church of the Holy Cross inside a pillar that bears the inscription *Gdzie skarb twój, tam i serce twoje* (For where thy treasure is, there is thy heart also (Matthew 6:21)).

The father of Polish opera: Stanisław Moniuszko

Poland's early encounters with opera tended to feature Italian compositions. *Nędza uszczęśliwiona* by Maciej Kamieński, first performed in 1778, is sometimes called the first native opera, although it was more like a play with a few songs thrown in. *Cud mniemany, czyli Krakowiacy i Górale* (1794) by Jan Stefani, stakes a more genuine claim, even whilst it wasn't of the highest quality.

In truth, it took the premiere of Stanisław Moniuszko's *Halka*, on January 1st 1858, to give Poland its first world-class opera, and the composer is indeed now commonly referred to as 'the father of Polish opera'. In *Halka*, a tragic tale of seduction, abandonment and suicide, Moniuszko created a truly national Romantic opera, incorporating native folk themes, dances and melodies. He wrote various other patriotic operas, the best probably being *Straszny dwór* (1865), the story of two brothers who vow to stay single in order to serve their country, but find themselves tempted astray in a supposedly haunted house.

Szymanowski stirs young Poland

Two Polish composers emerged from the rather tame crowd at the turn of the 20th century. The first was Władysław Żeleński, famous for operas such as *Goplana* (1896); the second, Ignacy Jan Paderewski, was an expert piano player who wrote one opera, *Manru* (1901), before turning his attention to politics, ultimately becoming Polish Prime Minister in 1919. It took the Young Poland movement to shake things up, inspiring a loose group of neo-Romantics who sought to reinvigorate artistic life. They succeeded, thanks to two figures in particular:

Mieczysław Karłowicz. The highly respected, mountain climbing author of gloomy, emotional symphonic poems, including *Odwieczne pieśni Op.10* (1906) and *Stanisław i Anna Oświecimowie Op.12* (1907). He was also one of the few Polish composers not to die of tuberculosis. Instead, he lost his life in an avalanche in the Tatra Mountains in 1909, aged 32.

Karol Szymanowski. Of wealthy stock and a well-known homosexual, Szymanowski is often regarded as second only to Chopin in the pantheon of Polish composers. He sought to free Polish music from the patriotic obsession instilled by Chopin and Moniuszko, looking instead to the wider concerns of the modern nation. In the subtly homoerotic opera *Król Roger* (1926) he explored the clash between Christianity and Paganism, whilst later works became imbued with the folk music and mythology of the Tatra Mountains, notably *Sinfonia Concertante Op. 60* (1932) and *Harnasie* (1931), a masterful ballet with a Robin Hood-esque lead.

Dissonant days: the post-war avant-garde

The cultural thaw that followed Stalin's death saw Polish classical music reasserting its authority. The founding of the Warsaw Autumn (Warszawska Jesień) festival in 1956 created a showcase for new talent, and a group of young avant-garde musicians known as the 'Polish Composers' School' emerged soon after. Some of the figures involved remain influential today.

The key avant-garde composers

Wojciech Kilar. Known for the disturbing, intensely Modernist *Riff 62* (1962), a great success at the Warsaw Autumn festival, and the symphonic poem, *Krzesany* (1974). Kilar is also famous for his film scores, notably *Dracula* (1992) and *The Pianist* (2002).

Unanimous indecision

In 1959 the Polish Composers' Union held a competition for young talent. The judges, having assessed 200 anonymously submitted entries, couldn't agree on the ordering of first, second and third prize. However, after much debate, a compromise was reached: they awarded one first prize and two equal second prizes. They needn't have bothered – when the entrant names were finally revealed, it turned out that Krzysztof Penderecki, then unknown, had composed all three of the top works.

Three more from the 20th century

Tadeusz Baird. The son of Scottish migrants, best known for *Cztery sonety miłosne* (1969).

Andrzej Panufnik. Defected to the UK in 1954, where he wrote *Katyń Epitaph* (1968).

Włodzimierz Kotoński. A forerunner in electronic music; *Etiuda na jedno uderzenie w talerz* (1959) broke new ground.

Soundtrack to your nightmares

Dracula (1992) was scored by Wojciech Kilar. *The Shining* (1980) and *The Exorcist* (1973) both used Krzysztof Penderecki's dissonant orchestral work *Polymorphia* (1961).

Krzysztof Penderecki. The pioneer of Sonorism – exploring the sonic possibilities of instruments (dropping them on the floor, for instance) – and one of the most performed 20th century Polish composers. His best work includes: *Tren 'Ofiarom Hiroszimy'* (1960), an experimental orchestral piece; and *Die Teufel von Loudun* (1969), an opera about demonic possession and exorcism.

Henryk Mikołaj Górecki. Górecki's early Modernist music was characterised by harsh, unsettling dissonance, as heard in *Symfonia nr 2 'Kopernikowska' Op. 31* (1972). Later he moved towards a more spiritual, minimalist sound, notably with *Symfonia nr 3 'Symfonia Pieśni Żałosnych' Op. 36* (1977). Górecki only became a household name when a London Sinfonietta recording of his Third Symphony was released in 1992 as *Symphony of Sorrowful Songs*. It sold over a million copies.

Witold Lutosławski. Lutosławski was a great experimenter, creating 12-tone music that used a predetermined sequence of all 12 notes in a strict order, and aleatory music, employing random procedures to determine the content and order of a composition. Intricate and emotional, *Wariacje na temat Paganiniego* (1941), *Muzyka żałobna* (1958) and *Symfonia nr 3* (1983) were three of his best.

Contemporary composers and audiences

Of the current crop of young Polish composers, the postmodern work of Paweł Mykietyn has found a receptive audience; *Sonety Shakespeare'a na sopran męski i fortepian* (2000) and the opera *Ignorant i szaleniec* (2001) were both well received. Paweł Szymański explores musical traditions placed in a modern setting, as in *A Kaleidoscope for M.C.E.* (1994), a tribute to Dutch artist Escher. Finally, Hanna Kulenty won plaudits with *Matka czarnoskrzydłych snów* (1995), a one-act opera about madness and heartbreak.

The relatively healthy state of 'new' classical music in Poland is matched by a reasonable appetite for live performance. Concerts and festivals are held nationwide; the Warsaw Autumn festival is still going, accompanied today by several other significant events, including the Misteria Paschalia, Wratislavia Cantans, Sacrum Profanum and Easter Beethoven festivals. The country is also home to several internationally respected orchestras, not least the Warsaw National Philharmonic Orchestra, established in 1901, and the National Polish Radio Symphony Orchestra in Katowice, dating from 1935.

Krzysztof Penderecki

Composer and conductor
Threnody to the Victims of Hiroshima
was his 1960 masterpiece.

4.1.2 Folk stories: traditional music

The most famous Polish folk tune is *Mazurek Dąbrowskiego* (*Dąbrowski's mazurka*), also known as *Jeszcze Polska nie zginęła* (*Poland is not yet lost*), with lyrics written by Józef Wybicki in 1797 set to a traditional mazurka melody. The song was adopted as Poland's national anthem in 1926.

Songs of work and love

Polish folk music found an international audience in the late 18th century when the polonaise and mazurka were all the rage in the ballrooms of Europe, whilst Chopin and Moniuszko later mined the nation's folk rhythms and melodies for their own compositions (see section 4.1.1). There were, of course, numerous other, less celebrated Polish traditions; the work, love and seasonal songs of the peasantry, passed down from generation to generation. They were painstakingly collected by ethnographer Oskar Kolberg in the 19th century; he listed them in *Lud* (1857-1890), which stretched to 30 volumes and featured some 12,000 examples of folk music within. In the 1930s, sound recordings were made of more than 24,000 Polish folk songs and tunes, only for every last recording to be destroyed in the Second World War.

Hand in hand with dance

Poland's folk dances, many dating back to the 17th century and beyond, are integral to the country's musical tradition. Each dance is accompanied by music of the same name – the polonaise, for example, is danced to the polonaise.

Mazur (Mazurka). A lively improvisational dance for couples in 3/4 time with a heavily accented second beat (one TWO three), from the Mazovia region in central Poland.

Kujawiak. A smooth, flowing dance for couples who spin and sway like 'grain in the wind' according to one commentator; rather like a slower version of the mazurka, and also from the Mazovia region.

Oberek. Another dance not dissimilar to the mazurka, albeit more energetic with quick steps and couples constantly spinning around the room.

Krakowiak. A fast galloping dance in 2/4 time, often performed in traditional costume; from the south of Poland, Kraków in particular.

Polonez (Polonaise). A graceful ceremonial dance in 3/4 time derived from the 17th century 'walking dance' *chodzony*; often performed at formal social functions. Another dance from Kraków.

Slave to the rhythms

In the years of post-war Communist rule, Polish folk culture was commandeered by the state and used to build the image of Poland as a proud and healthy peasant republic. Folk music lessons were introduced in schools – even bagpipe lessons were on the curriculum – and state-funded folk ensembles set up, notably Mazowsze and Śląsk, which presented prefabricated national folk culture stripped of regional variation. Even whilst the attendant music and dance was executed with great artistry, the imposition of a new, sanitised version of folk greatly hastened the demise of genuine traditions.

Folk reborn

In the 21st century, traditional Polish folk music has pulled back from the brink. The enthusiasm for its revival has been considerable, its renaissance important to the reclamation of national and regional identity. Traditions are being rebuilt having lapsed or been dismantled. However, only one could really be called a 'living tradition', having retained its continuity throughout the years of upheaval: the songs and dances of the *górale* (highlanders) of the Podhale region. Typically, the music of the *górale* features a string band of three violins and a cello, playing angular melodies and accompanied by the distinctive high-pitched 'open throat' singing known as *biały głos* (white voice), derived from the shepherds' calls to their flock. Complex,

Four important folk bands

Zespół Polski. A group that only uses authentic instruments to play traditional Polish folk songs and dances, and which features the very talented Maria Pomianowska.

Kroke. Formed in 1992 in Kraków, Kroke are one of the best-known exponents of Jewish music in Europe (Kroke is Yiddish for Kraków). They began playing klezmer music compositions (once widespread in Poland but virtually wiped out during the Second World War) but have since woven a range of other ethnic influences into their work.

Trebunie-Tutki. Popular family folk group from the Podhale region that play traditional *górale* music, sometimes in combination with other genres.

Kapela ze wsi Warszawa (aka the Warsaw Village Band). Founded in 1997, Kapela ze wsi Warszawa successfully combine traditional Polish songs and instrumentation with modern beats and production techniques.

energetic dances accompany the music. Today, inevitably, they're performed for tourists as much as locals.

Beyond the Podhale region, most Poles will know a handful of traditional songs. Usually, they appear at wedding ceremonies: the famous *Sto lat* wishes for a long life (one hundred years to be exact); *Rośnie trawka* is sung at the unveiling (*oczepiny*); and *Spadła z wiśni* is used as a celebratory drinking song.

In the years since 1989, a number of popular folk bands have formed, repackaging Poland's musical heritage for a new audience. Many have achieved commercial success, and today the country stages several acclaimed folk festivals, including the Festival of Folk Bands and Singers (Festiwal Kapel i Śpiewaków Ludowych), in Kazimierz, and the International Folk Music Festival (Mikołajki Folkowe) in Lublin.

Going underground

Jazz came to Poland in the 1920s with the American jazz and swing craze that swept continental Europe after the First World War. Homegrown orchestras, such as those led by Jerzy Petersburski and Artur Gold, became hugely popular until, in 1939, the German invasion brought things to an abrupt halt. The 'decadent' syncopated rhythms remained banned in the years after the war, forcing jazz underground where it flourished at small, secret gatherings. Melomani, a band founded by saxophonist Jerzy 'Duduś' Matuszkiewicz, and with a distinctly fluid membership, led the way. The cultural thaw of the mid 1950s brought jazz back above ground, and it hasn't really looked back since. The first official jazz festival was at Sopot in 1956, then came clubs like the Stodoła in Warsaw, followed by an explosion of creativity in the 1960s and 70s. Avant-garde and free jazz thrived, pioneered by artists who would achieve international acclaim – and many of whom are still playing today.

Tomasz Stanko
World class jazz trumpet player.
In a class of his own.

Five giants of Polish jazz

Krzysztof Komeda. The influential pianist/composer and one-time member of Melomani, who enjoyed a successful but short career, dying aged 37 in 1969. Komeda only released one album in his lifetime, the revered *Astigmatic* (1965). The Komeda Jazz Festival in Słupsk is held each year in his memory.

Tomasz Stańko. An avant-garde trumpet player whose international reputation has endured for nearly 50 years. His haunting, lyrical style can be accessible and disturbing in equal measure. Try *Music for K* (1970) and *Dark Eyes* (2009).

Leszek Możdżer. Pianist Możdżer first rose to prominence in the early 1990s playing in the band Miłość. Has collaborated with the likes of Jon Schofield, Behemoth (see section 4.1.4) and David Gilmour.

Michał Urbaniak. An internationally renowned jazz violinist who came to prominence with *Fusion* (1974) and who incorporates elements as diverse as folk and hip-hop into his music.

Adam Makowicz. A virtuoso jazz pianist regarded as being among the best in the world. His technical ability and graceful style can be heard on *Live Embers* (1973) and *Reflections on Chopin* (2000).

Mummy's curse

Roman Polanski's film, *Rosemary's Baby* (1968), in which a young woman gives birth to the antichrist, has often been called 'cursed' because of the tragedy that befell the director's heavily pregnant wife, Sharon Tate, a year after the film was released. She was brutally murdered by members of Charles Manson's 'family'. However, few know of the movie's additional grim parallel: Krzysztof Komeda, composer of the film's score (he scored several films for Polanski), died in the same year after sustaining a head injury and falling into a coma – echoing the fate of another character in the film.

Jazz comes in from the cold

When the Iron Curtain came down, Poland's jazz scene was further invigorated by new record labels, such as Polonia Records, and by an increase in the number of foreign jazz artists touring the country. Miłość emerged as an important group in the 1990s with a new form of jazz they liked to call 'Yass' – a synthesis of free jazz, rock, punk and all sorts. *Talkin' About Life and Death* (1999) was a lauded Miłość album. Other contemporary artists of note have included the Simple Acoustic Trio, reimagined more recently as the Marcin Wasilewski (the pianist) Trio, with their highly acclaimed album *Lyrics* (2001); and Skalpel, a duo of DJ/producer whose sampling and reworking of Polish jazz history, on albums such as *Konfusion* (2005), has brought critical and commercial success. Poland's jazz festivals, notably the Jazz Jamboree in Warsaw and the Summer Jazz Festival (Letni Festiwal Jazzowy) in Kraków, are reliably well attended.

Hail! Hail! Rock 'n' roll

When Elvis was in his early pomp, changing the face of Western music, Poland was at its lowest cultural ebb, and any homegrown imitation stood little chance of success. However, a poppy, derivative Polish version of rock 'n' roll did emerge in the 1960s, inspired by American and British bands. Dubbed Big Beat *(mocne uderzenie)*, young Poles loved it, and popular music established a permanent place in the country's culture. It would always be something the older generation (and the ruling authorities) didn't understand; it gave young Poles an escape, an arena in which they could explore emotional, political and social freedom.

Czesław Niemen, a charismatic singer/songwriter, was the first artist to sound a public note of dissent. He wrote *Dziwny jest ten świat* (1967), a protest song on a big-selling album of the same name. With his powerful vocal style, Nieman became (and remains) an iconic figure in Poland; the psychedelic(ish) *Enigmatic* (1970) is usually considered to be his best album.

A flavour of modern Polish music: ten albums

Ewa Demarczyk śpiewa piosenki Zygmunta Koniecznego (1967) Ewa Demarczyk

Enigmatic (1970) Czesław Niemen

Blues (1971) Breakout

Nocny Patrol (1983) Maanam

Brygada Kryzys (1983) Brygada Kryzys

Nowe sytuacje (1983) Republika

Poligono Industrial (2005) Kult

L Niño vol. 1 (2006) Liroy

Happiness is Easy (2006) Myslovitz

On My Own (2007) Tatiana Okupnik

"STRANGE IS THIS WORLD WHERE THERE IS SO MUCH EVIL"
From *Dziwny jest ten świat* by Czesław Niemen

Three Big Beat bands and their albums

Czerwono-Czarni: *Czerwono-Czarni* (1966). The first band in Poland to cut a record.

Niebiesko-Czarni: *Mamy dla was kwiaty* (1968). Supported the Rolling Stones in 1967.

Czerwone Gitary: *To właśnie my* (1966). 'The Polish Beatles'.

Stoned and gassed

On 13th April 1967, the Rolling Stones played two concerts to a carefully selected audience at the Palace of Culture and Science in Warsaw. Outside, the police fired teargas into the ticketless crowd laying siege to the building. The Stones were the first Western rock 'n' roll band to play behind the Iron Curtain.

Anarchy in Poland

Fanaberia (2002) Blue Café

Diamond Bitch (2007) Doda

Feel (2007) Feel

Natalia Lesz (2008) Natalia Lesz

Boso (2011) Zakopower

One hit wonder

Ewa Demarczyk, known as the 'Black Angel', is widely regarded as the most talented and charismatic of all Polish singers; an artist whose dramatic, emotional style, reminiscent of a Polish (and female) Jacques Brel, still resonates today. Remarkably, however, Demarczyk only released one studio album in Polish: *Ewa Demarczyk śpiewa piosenki Zygmunta Koniecznego* (1967) (she released a Russian language version in 1974 and a live album in 1982).

Brygada Kryzys. Punk band formed from the ashes of Kryzys and Tilt by frontman Tomek Lipiński. They were banned after refusing to headline a state-organised concert.

Republika. New wave band that used rich metaphor to get around the censor.

Maanam. Post-punk, new-wavish band fronted by female singer Kora. One particular song (and album), *Nocny Patrol* (1983), captured the mid '80s mood.

Kult. An underground rock band whose direct lyrics found censorship but which went on to achieve great success in the post-Communist era.

TSA. Hard-to-ignore band that brought together the accoutrements of hard rock (long hair, sweaty torsos, etc) with invective for the regime.

The 1970s ushered in a number of rock bands, notably Budka Suflera, still going strong today more than three decades on from their first album, *Cień wielkiej góry* (1975). The Hendrix/Cream influenced sound of Breakout, formed by Tadeusz Nalepa, was similarly popular. Late in the decade, with meagre collective and personal freedom and an economy in freefall, the spirit of Czesław Niemen returned, reborn in punk, a movement that epitomised perfectly the frustrations of Poland's youth. A Warsaw band called Tilt led the way.

Against the backdrop of martial law, strikes, shortages and inflation, Polish music boomed in the 1980s, giving voice to the generation that considered itself 'lost'. Bands had to pass their lyrics in front of the censor; if the words met with approval, the artists could enter the recording studio. Many bands simply altered their lyrics for live shows, aware that the security services in attendance at most gigs would have little understanding of what they were singing. Audience members would record the shows and then circulate illicit audiotapes. Equally, with the authorities preoccupied elsewhere, music events could often pass with relatively little interference; indeed, some were even encouraged by the state, organised as a 'diversion' from the mounting street protests.

Contemporary sounds

From the 1990s onwards, popular Polish music, unfettered by censorship and inevitably less politicised, evolved along familiar lines:

Rock music is still popular, played by the likes of punk/folk/indie band Lao Che, acclaimed for *Powstanie Warszawskie* (2005), and Myslovitz, intelligent indie rockers whose albums *Happiness is Easy* (2006) and *Nieważne jak wysoko jesteśmy...* (2011), both topped the Polish charts.

Heavy metal (and its extreme offshoots, death and black metal) has been hugely popular since the late 1980s. Turbo are a big name, acclaimed for the album *Kawaleria Szatana* (1987), as are Decapitated (*Nihility* (2002)), Newbreed (*The New Way of Human Existence* (2002)) and Behemoth (*Evangelion* (2009)). Vader are Poland's most successful death metal band, the force behind *Litany* (2000) and *The Beast* (2004).

Dance music in its many forms emerged in the 1990s with Disco Polo, a folk-based dance music that rapidly evolved into the cheesier 'Euro disco'. Shazza lit the fire with a huge hit, *Bierz co chcesz* (1995). In recent years, trance and techno have grown in popularity with artists such as Kalwi & Remi (*Kiss Me Girl* (2011)) and Wet Fingers, and are experienced at big events like the Sunrise Festival in Kołobrzeg.

Rap has spawned Płomień 81, whose third album, *Historie z sąsiedztwa* (2005), is probably his best; and Liroy, Poland's biggest rapper, who has enjoyed a string of big-selling albums, including the hugely successful *Albóóm* (1995).

Poland's Woodstock

Free-spirited music festivals weren't the norm in the Eastern Bloc. Indeed, the annual Jarocin Festival, first held in 1980 in the small Wielkopolska town of the same name, was in a minority of one. The event attracted 20,000 or more young music lovers each year throughout the 1980s. They came to listen to bands that couldn't make it past the censors onto radio or TV (or even the recording studio). Secret police officers mingled with the hippies, rockers and punks.

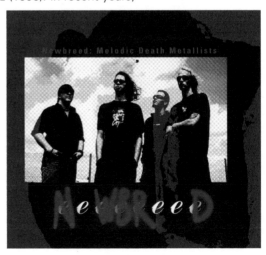

125

4.2 Theatre and comedy

For centuries, Poland struggled to find its own dramatic tradition. When it arrived, the great playwrights used folklore, metaphor and subversion to put Poland itself centre stage.

1. Identity: the
foundations
of Polish culture

2. Literature
and philosophy

3. Art, architecture
and design

**4. Music, theatre,
and comedy**

5. Cinema
and fashion

6. Media and
communications

7. Food and drink

8. Living culture:
the state of
modern Poland

Biblical background: the medieval mystery plays

Poland's theatrical tradition reaches back to the religious dramas of the Middle Ages. The clergy performed in Latin, perhaps aware that their audience was more likely to grasp the subject matter if

it was acted out. Gradually, these dramas developed into morality and mystery plays, performed in the vernacular in market squares. The most famous surviving play of the era is an Easter mystery play, *Historyja o chwalebnym zmartwychwstaniu Pańskim (The History of the Glorious Resurrection of Our Lord)*, written down in 1570 by Mikołaj z Wilkowiecka, a monk from Częstochowa, but dating from the 1400s.

Renaissance home truths

The classical dramas of the Renaissance, with their secular content, seeped into Polish theatre in the early 16th century, and the rediscovered plays of Seneca, Plautus and Terence were performed in Latin at the royal court in Kraków. Vernacular translations followed, performances spread to other noble courts and homegrown Renaissance drama began to appear. The landmark work was a tragedy, *Odprawa posłów greckich (The Dismissal of the Greek Envoys)* by Jan Kochanowski, the dramatist perhaps more famous as a poet (see section 2.1.2). Performed first for the king and queen in 1578, ostensibly *Odprawa posłów greckich* was a play about the self-interest and infighting of the Trojan court, yet it carried a clear warning about the fate of contemporary Poland. Such allegory would prove a popular device for Polish playwrights in the centuries to come.

Highbrow imports and homemade humour

The nascent native drama of the Renaissance was lost amid the translations of Italian opera and French plays that grew popular in the royal and noble courts of the 17th century. Amongst the imports, Baroque poet Jan Andrzej Morsztyn's vernacular rendering of Pierre Corneille's *Le Cid* was celebrated, and remains the standard version in Poland today. Beyond the courts, however, a more homespun theatrical tradition evolved. The unsophisticated *komedia rybałtowska* featured travelling troupes of players performing popular, coarse dramas in the town squares and market places. The most popular comedy was *Z chłopa król* (*The Peasant King*) (1637), Piotr Baryka's tale about a peasant who gets so drunk he thinks he's a king.

Ribaldry from the rybalts

The itinerant *komedia rybałtowska* of the 17th century didn't take its name from the 'ribald' nature of the drama. It seems more likely that the 'rybalts' were the authors of the comedic skits. Apparently, they were often local teachers fallen on hard times, writing satire to bring in some money.

4.2.2 Plays in Polish: Enlightenment and Romantic dramas

Founding a National Theatre

Under King Stanisław August Poniatowski, Polish theatre gained its own identity. In 1765 he established the National Theatre (Teatr Narodowy) in Warsaw, for which Polish actors performed Polish plays. The key figure in the National Theatre's early years was Wojciech Bogusławski, an actor, playwright and director who drove the institution's Enlightenment-led repertoire of patriotic drama. Three playwrights in particular built their reputations on works staged at the National Theatre:

Franciszek Bohomolec. A Jesuit priest who juxtaposed the old Polish nobility with modern, enlightened figures. His best work was *Małżeństwo z kalendarza (Marriage by the Calendar)* (1766), a satirical take on superstition.

Franciszek Zabłocki. The prime author of comedic drama in the Polish Enlightenment wrote *Fircyk w zalotach (The Dandy's Courtship)* (1781), a satire in relatively colloquial language.

Julian Ursyn Niemcewicz. The reformist politician authored *Powrót posła (The Return of the Envoy)* (1791), an influential political comedy ridiculing the nobility.

Comedy in the age of national tragedy

The great Romantic Polish poets, Mickiewicz, Słowacki, Krasiński and Norwid (see section 2.1.4 for details on all four), wrote their 'closet dramas' (many of which actually took to the stage years later) in exile, whilst back in early 19th century Poland, playwrights found themselves – like their country – stripped of independence. There was strict censorship, particularly in the Russian-occupied territories, and yet Polish dramatists continued to produce fine work, even if it lacked the revolutionary bent of the Romantic émigrés. Aleksander Fredro was the major playwright. He modelled his plays on those of Molière and Goldoni, and was duly acclaimed for the rich characterisation and fine construction evident in his comedies. Many depicted life in the Polish gentry: *Mąż i żona (Man and Wife)* (1822) was a tale of marital infidelity, and *Zemsta (Vengeance)* (1834), concerning the disputed ownership of a castle, is considered to be his masterpiece.

Aleksander Fredo

Polanski does Fredro

Aleksander Fredro's hugely popular farce, *Zemsta*, was adapted for the big screen in 2002. Much of the original plot and dialogue were retained for the film, which starred Roman Polanski in the role of Papkin.

The star of two continents

The great actors of the 19th century became the first stars of the stage. In Poland, Leontyna Halpertowa was famed for her ability and looks, but for Helena Modjeska (sometimes it was Modrzejewska, even though neither were her real name), the renown spread across continents. Her Shakespearean roles were celebrated in Europe and the USA, where she eventually took up citizenship. In noting Helena's achievements on the centenary of her death, the modern Polish parliament recently described her as 'the star of two continents'.

4.2.3 Experimental intermission:
the interwar years

Wyspiański's Wesele

The influence of Stanisław Wyspiański's *Wesele* (translated into English as *The Wedding*, although *The Wedding Reception* would be more accurate) on Polish cultural life in the 20th century was huge. A number of phrases from the play's dialogue passed into common usage. 'Golden horn' became a metaphor for lost hopes, whilst 'Straw man dance' described something powerful yet illusory.

Young Poland on stage

Polish theatre rather drifted through the later 19th century, the highlights shaped by actors rather than playwrights (who were still stifled by Tsarist censorship). It took the Young Poland movement to reinvigorate drama (and the other arts) at the turn of the 20th century. Stanisław Wyspiański, painter (see section 3.1.2), poet, stained glass window maker and playwright, was the leading light. He married Modernist lighting and staging techniques with old Polish folklore in a series of patriotic plays. *Wesele (The Wedding)* (1901) was considered Wyspiański's best work. It's a tale of stagnation and wasted opportunity, set at a wedding where the guests are visited by the ghosts of Poland past. The innovative, symbolic finale is a wordless scene, the actors performing a slow dreamlike dance like puppets controlled from above. Two subsequent Wyspiański plays, *Wyzwolenie (Liberation)* (1903); *Noc listopadowa (November Night)* (1904), also remain in the Polish repertoire.

Introspective flourish

Between the wars, theatre flourished in newly independent Poland. New theatres were founded in cities across the country – Poland had 32 by 1938 – whilst travelling companies, such as Reduta, an experimental group under the direction of Juliusz Osterwa, toured the provinces. Freed from the crusade for national independence, dramatists turned to more personal and social themes. Jerzy Szaniawski was popular, the author of comedies that fused everyday reality with more introspective, philosophical themes. *Ptak* (*The Bird*) (1923), first directed by Juliusz Osterwa, was typical. Szaniawski is best remembered for *Dwa teatry* (*Two Theatres*) (1946), a play within a play.

The mad genius of Witkacy

The work of another interwar playwright, Stanisław Ignacy Witkiewicz (or Witkacy as he liked to call himself) were largely ignored in his own lifetime, and only found acclaim on their rediscovery in the 1950s, when they influenced avant-garde theatre. Born in Warsaw but educated at home (where he wrote his first play, *Karaluchy* (*Cockroaches*) (1893) aged eight) in Zakopane, near the Czech border, by his painter father, Witkacy was also an artist, novelist, philosopher and experimenter with narcotics. His plays were characterised by illogical plots and grotesque humour. He created visions of a doomed, mad world, rejecting traditional technique and instead advocating *Czysta Forma*, his theory of 'Pure Form' that demanded drama provoke a debate on human existence, like 'the brain of a madman presented on stage'. Two Witkacy plays in particular remain important:

Bones of contention
On September 18th 1939, on learning that Soviet troops were advancing into Poland from the East, Witkacy committed suicide by taking a drug overdose. He was buried in the town where he died, in the churchyard at Jeziory, now in Ukraine. However, in what could pass for the plot of one of his plays, the body was apparently dug up by the Communist authorities in 1950, with no one being allowed to look inside the coffin, and reburied in Zakopane. When the remains were exhumed once more in 1994, this time by the Ministry of Culture and Art, the re-interred body was found to be that of an unknown woman.

Mątwa (*The Cuttlefish*) (1922). An alienated artist becomes an absolute dictator.

Wariat i zakonnica (*The Madman and the Nun*) (1923). The story of a love affair between a poet and a nun in a lunatic asylum, in which two characters who die on stage reappear unharmed later on in the play.

Schiller sets a new direction

The great director of Poland's interwar flourish was Leon Schiller, whose Modernist 'monumental theatre' productions of works by the great Romantic poets, particularly (before it was banned again) Mickiewicz's patriotic, mystical drama, *Dziady* (*Forefather's Eve*) at Warsaw's Teatr Polski in 1934, brought great fame and went some way to establish the predominance of the director in Polish theatre, a primacy which endures to the present day.

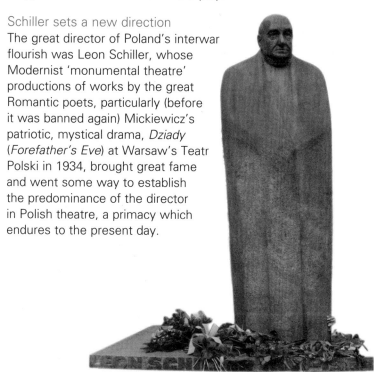

Absurd post-war truths

After the Second World War, Polish theatre was regulated by the Soviet-controlled Ministry of Art and Culture. Plays deemed subversive, such as those by the Romantic poets, were forbidden and theatres were expected to produce drama that conformed to the tenets of Socialist Realism (*socrealizm*), exploring in particular the collective joys of working in a factory. Unsurprisingly, the results were poor. Following the death of Stalin, the Polish government gained autonomy over the arts, and liberal state funding from the mid 1950s onwards generated a flowering of creativity. Compromises were inevitably made – strict censorship forbade social or political commentary – and yet a number of internationally acclaimed plays were written, many in the form of Absurdist, avant-garde works that the censors didn't understand. Metaphor and allusion were used – as they had been as far back as the Renaissance – to spotlight Poland's plight, however obliquely.

The role of Alternative Theatre

'Alternative Theatre' played a small but significant role in defying the post-war Communist authorities. Some were tiny: the Tarczyńska Street Theatre (Teatr na Tarczyńskiej) founded in 1953, constituted a small gathering in writer Miron Białoszewski's flat. Others, such as student groups like STS, Bim-Bom and the renowned Theatre of the Eighth Day (Teatr Ósmego Dnia) had more impact. Set up in 1964, the Theatre of the Eighth Day was routinely censored and banned, and targeted and framed by the secret police, and yet somehow created politicised, avant-garde theatre for more than 20 years. *Piołun* (*Wormwood*) (1985) was their most famous play. Having left Poland in 1988, the Theatre of the Eighth Day is now back performing in the country.

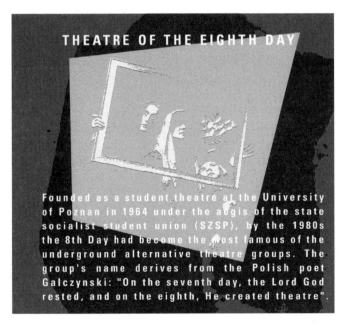

THEATRE OF THE EIGHTH DAY

Founded as a student theatre at the University of Poznan in 1964 under the aegis of the state socialist student union (SZSP), by the 1980s the 8th Day had become the most famous of the underground alternative theatre groups. The group's name derives from the Polish poet Galczynski: "On the seventh day, the Lord God rested, and on the eighth, He created theatre".

In 1947, the new Polish Ministry of Culture and Art sponsored a nationwide Shakespeare Festival, featuring 17 of the English playwright's works, performed across 23 theatres. Leon Schiller took first prize in the festival competition with a production of *The Tempest*. Even while the use of 'Western' playwrights declined soon after the festival, Shakespeare was still regularly performed in Soviet-controlled Poland, the content of his plays somehow reinterpreted as a farsighted forecast of Marxist theory. Conversely, many of the directors and companies used Shakespeare's plays to subtly criticise the regime.

Five key post-war playwrights

Witold Gombrowicz. A well-known novelist (see section 2.1.5), and the most performed Polish playwright, Gombrowicz wrote largely in exile, in Argentina. His highly influential grotesque plays were banned in Poland until after his death in 1969. Gombrowicz' characters inhabit an absurd fairytale world in which they battle with each other and against what is expected of them. *Iwona Księżniczka Burgunda* (*Yvonne, the Princess of Burgundy*) (1935) portrays the murder of an ugly girl chosen by a prince to be his bride for a joke; whilst his most famous play, *Ślub* (*The Wedding*) (1946), features a dream, a human sacrifice and a marriage that doesn't take place.

Tadeusz Różewicz. An acclaimed poet, as well as the author of experimental, dreamlike plays that employed 'open dramaturgy', encouraging contributions from the director and cast. Różewicz is celebrated for *Kartoteka* (*The Card Index*) (1968), featuring a nameless character disillusioned by the post-war government; and *Białe małżeństwo* (*White Wedding*) (1975), a deceptively conventional play about the sexual awakening of two girls in a small Polish town.

Sławomir Mrożek. The writer of absurd, macabre dramas who left Poland for France and Mexico in 1963 (resulting in a ban on his works for some years), returning in the 1990s, and who earned international acclaim with plays such as *Tango* (1964), about idealism, despotism and family conflict, and *Emigranci* (*The Emigrants*) (1974), telling of an intellectual and a peasant, both emigrants to Paris, who have only their disillusionment in common.

Jerzy Szaniawski. An acclaimed short story writer who also authored plays both pre- and post-war. Many were satirical; most had an everyday setting. *Dwa teatry* (*Two Theatres*) (1946), in which, typically, the regular events of life conceal dreams and longings, was his most acclaimed work.

Leon Kruczkowski. Another novelist-cum-playwright, Kruczkowski worked within the state's cultural framework after the war (indeed, he was the Deputy Minister for Culture and Art). He wrote *Niemcy* (*Germans*) (1949), set in occupied Poland, Norway and France in 1943, capturing the tense atmosphere of daily life amid denouncements and reprisals.

The rise of the directors

The importance of the theatre director grew in Poland (as it did elsewhere) throughout the second half of the 20th century. The likes of Józef Szajna, an Auschwitz survivor who created highly visual 'art theatre' often led by his wartime memories, and Krystian Lupa, proved highly influential and earned international acclaim. Two others, in particular, have stuck in the collective memory:

Tadeusz Kantor. Kantor came to prominence in the 1950s with revolutionary set designs. He used mannequins as actors and stages that reached out into the audience, and created 'happenings' under the auspices of his avant-garde company, Cricot 2. Kantor is best known for staging work by Witkacy, and for his own *Umarła klasa* (*Dead Class*) (1975), which features a teacher and a class of seemingly dead students.

Jerzy Grotowski. An influential figure in late 20th century theatre, Grotowski first made his name with experimental theatre in the 1960s, produced with his company the Laboratory Theatre (Teatr Laboratorium). He devised the concept of 'Poor Theatre', as detailed in his book, *Ku teatrowi ubogiemu* (*Towards a Poor Theatre*) (1968), which emphasised the relationship between audience and actor, and advocated dispensing with any unnecessary distractions – like props, make up, costume, sound, lighting... or a script.

TADEUSZ
KANTOR
REŻYSER

A new breed of writers

The authority of the director in Polish theatre has continued to grow in the 21ˢᵗ century. In recent years, debate has surfaced about whether this rise has been at the expense of new writers who, some argue, have been largely ignored. However, even while new directors such as Jan Klata and Maja Kleczewska continue to grab the limelight, the lot of the Polish playwright has improved considerably of late. A number of exciting new writers have emerged:

Dorota Masłowska. A writer (see section 2.1.6) whose first play, *Dwoje biednych Rumunów mówiących po polsku* (*A Couple of Poor, Polish-Speaking Romanians*) (2006) passed comment on wealth and poverty in contemporary Poland, using a pair of hitch-hiking oddballs who aren't all they appear to be. The play was well received internationally.

Małgorzata Sikorska-Miszczuk. Acclaimed for works of 'depressive feminism' such as *Szajba* (*Loose Screws*) (2007), an absurdist political drama featuring Islamic separatists in Poland.

Tadeusz Słobodzianek. Winner of the prestigious NIKE Award in 2010 for *Nasza Klasa* (*Our Class*) (2008), a play about Polish-Jewish relations before, during and after the Second World War.

Drama rooted in reality: the current state of theatre
Theatre has long held an important place in Poland's
cultural history, often reflecting the social and political
troubles the country has faced over the centuries, and
it retains a significant role today. However, even whilst
the collapse of the Communist regime lifted the shackles
of censorship, some have suggested that Polish theatre
has actually regressed over the last two decades. Indeed,
they talk of crisis. Of the 60 or so previously state-funded
repertory companies in the country, only around a dozen
now receive government financing (the National Theatre,
still going strong after nearly 250 years, is amongst them).
The rest must pay their own way. Theatre attendances
fell by 50 per cent between 1988 and 1994, although their
subsequent levelling off suggests that Polish theatre may
actually be coming to terms with the unpleasant reality
that there are too many repertory companies for a nation
of this size. Equally, current attendance figures may
indicate the true level of popularity now that cheap, if not
free, state-subsidised tickets and union block bookings
are a thing of the past.

1. Identity: the
foundations
of Polish culture

2. Literature
and philosophy

3. Art, architecture
and design

**4. Music, theatre,
and comedy**

5. Cinema
and fashion

6. Media and
communications

7. Food and drink

8. Living culture:
the state of
modern Poland

No fool like an old fool

Stańczyk, the 16th century jester at the royal court, was famously portrayed in Jan Matejko's painting of 1862, which shows him distraught at the news of a military defeat while the rest of the royal party dances the night away. Stańczyk would reappear at the start of the 20th century as one of the ghosts of Poland's past in Stanisław Wyspiański's influential play, *Wesele* (*The Wedding*) (1901), a satire on the politics and morals of the day.

A love of cabaret

Comedy plays a considerable role in the cultural life of Poland. Indeed, the country has a comedic tradition reaching back to the Renaissance courts of the 16th century, when Stańczyk, jester to the royals, was

renowned for ridiculing the real fools – namely Kings Aleksander, Zygmunt I, and Zygmunt II – with apparent impunity. In more recent times, Polish comedy found its strongest audience in cabaret. The enlightened years of the early 20th century ushered in the cabaret clubs, beginning with Krakow's Zielony Balonik (meaning 'little green balloon'), founded in 1905, where satirical sketches and monologues were performed for a select audience. Others, such as Momus in Warsaw, followed soon after; their doors open to a wider public and their routines more risqué. From the 1920s onwards, many of the clubs began including comedy films in their programmes. Notable among the interwar cabaret artistes

were Kazimierz Krukowski and Adolf Dymsza, a hugely popular comedy duo that performed under the name of Lopek and Florek throughout the 1920s and 30s in the Qui Pro Quo in Warsaw.

Adolf Dymsza

TV, cabaret and stand-up: a contemporary comedy diet
In the latter years of the 20th century, television became an increasingly important host to Polish comedy. Stanislaw Bareja's 1983 series *Alternatywy 4* (*4, Alternative Street*) was popular, using an assortment of characters living in the same house as a device for political satire. The sketch show series *Za chwilę dalszy ciąg programu* (*This Show Will Return in a Moment*) was equally well received in the early 1990s. Today, television remains a major platform for comedy. In 2006, Comedy Central Poland was launched, broadcasting imported as well as home-grown programmes, including *Włatcy móch* (a misspelled *Lord of the Flies*), the popular, irreverent adult cartoon show featuring a group of very strange eight-year-old schoolboys.

Cabaret remains the most popular form of live comedy. Typically, it features a group of four of five comedians who present sketches with bizarre characters in costume (men dressed as women, figures from history, etc). Kabaret Ani Mru Mru, Kabaret LIMO and Kabaret DNO are amongst the best known. The country retains a good number of clubs and small theatres venues such as Kraków's Rotunda Theatre, host of the annual PAKA cabaret competition. Stand-up comedy is a relatively new phenomenon in a country that has traditionally laughed at satire and buffoonery. However, acts like Kacper Ruciński and Katarzyna Piasecka are gaining an audience through observational humour, and TV stand-up shows, such as *Zabij mnie śmiechem* (*Stand up. Kill Me with Laughter*), grow in popularity.

5 Cinema and fashion

5.1 Cinema

Poland has a special relationship with cinema. Where other artists were stifled by the post-war cultural clampdown, filmmakers successfully found ways to express their creativity. A generation of inspiring directors emerged, establishing a tradition of expressive, complex cinema that draws on the country's turbulent history.

1. Identity: the foundations of Polish culture

2. Literature and philosophy

3. Art, architecture and design

4. Music, theatre, and comedy

5. Cinema and fashion

6. Media and communications

7. Food and drink

8. Living culture: the state of modern Poland

5.1.1 Bugs, epics and shtetls: the dawn of Polish cinema

Shots from the front

Having invented the Pleograph, in 1909 Kazimierz Prószyński moved on to the Aeroscope, a handheld camera powered by compressed air. The reel of film inside turned automatically, freeing the user from continually rotating a crank. In particular, the manoeuvrable Aeroscope lent itself well to another new wonder of the age, air travel, and was used by pilots in the First World War to photograph the battlefields below. Prószyński continued inventing after the First World War, although couldn't reproduce his earlier success. When the Nazis invaded Poland they hounded him, suspicious of his activities. He was eventually arrested amid the Warsaw Uprising of 1944, and died in Mauthausen concentration camp two months before its liberation.

Moving with the times: the early pioneers

Poland was quick to embrace film. Even whilst the Lumière brothers were stealing the limelight with their cinematograph in Paris, in 1894 Kazimierz Prószyński, an inventor in Warsaw, patented the Pleograph, a camera that shot and projected moving images. By 1899, Poland had its first cinema – in Łódź – and several more followed soon after. Prószyński made some of the first films, documentaries that left audiences astonished at their depiction of everyday activities such as ice-skating. Another Polish pioneer, Bolesław Matuszewski, used the Lumières' equipment whilst filming diplomatic visits in St Petersburg, as commissioned by Tsar Nicholas II.

Dead insects and historical epics

The first Polish feature film was released in 1908. Antoni Fertner, a popular cabaret artist, directed and starred in *Antoś pierwszy raz w Warszawie* (*Antos For The First Time in Warsaw*), a short farce about a country yokel who pitches up in the capital. Sequels followed and Fertner became the first star of Polish cinema. However, the first filmmaker of any critical depth was Władysław Starewicz. Born in Russia to Polish parents (he never actually lived in Poland proper), he was an animator; a pioneer in 'stop-motion' films that often made use of dead insects, repositioned frame-by-frame to create the narrative. Starewicz' most popular early film was *Mest' kinematograficheskogo operatora* (*The Cameraman's Revenge*) (1912), in which an adulterous stag beetle and a grasshopper (the cameraman of the title) fall out in a nightclub. He continued making animated movies into the 1960s. Much of Poland's remaining early film repertoire adapted literary or theatrical classics, particularly those that lobbied for the Polish cause, such as *Kościuszko pod Racławicami* (*Kościuszko at Racławicami*) (1913), taken from a play about General Kościuszko's heroic defeat against the Russians (see section 1.2.2).

Silent movies and the great Jewish filmmakers

The reinstatement of Poland's sovereignty after the First World War spurred the cinematic celebration of nationhood, and the adaptation of patriotic plays, operas and novels continued. Henryk Szaro was a leading director in the last years of the silent era. *Mocny człowiek* (*The Strong Man*) (1929), in which a journalist kills off his friend and makes good with the dead man's unpublished manuscript, was one of his most successful films. Like many of Poland's leading interwar filmmakers, Szaro made the switch from silent films to talkies. And, again like several contemporary directors, Szaro was Jewish, and shot some of his films in Yiddish. Eventually he would die in the Warsaw Ghetto in 1942.

Leave out the lip synch

Another Jewish director, Michał Waszyński, did most to capture the vivacity of Poland's pre-war Jewish population, shooting *Der Dibuk* (*The Dybbuk*) (1937), a traditional story that evoked the feel of a typical Polish shtetl. However, another director, Joseph Green, a Pole born Yoysef Grinberg who took American citizenship in the 1920s, produced Poland's most seen Yiddish film, *Yidl Mitn Fidl* (*Yiddle With His Fiddle*) (1936), a musical shot in Kazimierz, Kraków's historic Jewish district, and starring American actress, Molly Picon.

Polish audiences in the early years of talkies hated watching dubbed films. Indeed, the only foreign language film to top the box office in the interwar years was Disney's *Snow White and the Seven Dwarfs* (1937), a triumph that might owe more to the Poles' love of animation than to the film itself.

Star qualities: Pola Negri

The big star of early Polish cinema was Pola Negri. Born Barbara Apolonia Chałupiec in Lipno in 1897, she appeared in her first film, *Niewolnica zmysłów* (*Slave to her Senses*), in 1914 and rapidly became a Europe-wide star. A move to Berlin followed, where Charlie Chaplin saw Pola on screen and returned to the USA raving about her talents. By 1922 she was in Hollywood and two years later scored her first big American success in *Forbidden Paradise* (1924). However, a reputation for mild wantonness – Rod le Rocque and Rudolph Valentino were amongst her lovers – meant the work in America dried up and Negri returned to Europe, first to Paris and then to Berlin, where she became the darling of the Nazi elite – a French magazine alleged an affair with Hitler but she successfully sued. She ended up back in the USA, making infrequent films through to her death in 1987.

147

1. Identity: the foundations of Polish culture
2. Literature and philosophy
3. Art, architecture and design
4. Music, theatre, and comedy
5. Cinema and fashion
6. Media and communications
7. Food and drink
8. Living culture: the state of modern Poland

5.1.2 Wajda bends the rules

'MR. FORD, KEEP
THEM COMING!'
New York Times review
of Aleksander Ford's *Five
Boys from Barska Street*

Anti (social) hero
Having initially thrown
his creative talents into
making films for the
Communists, by the late
1950s Aleksander Ford
had lost his enthusiasm
for the regime. In 1968
he was accused of
'antisocial' activity by
the state, based on a
film he'd made a decade
earlier, *Ósmy dzien
tygodnia* (*Eighth Day
of the Week*) (1958),
which painted a rather
gloomy portrait of
contemporary Poland.
Refusing to apologise,
Ford was expelled from
the Communist party
and fled the country,
eventually settling in
the USA. In Poland he
became a 'non-person'
and any recognition of
his work was terminated,
as noted in the famous,
clandestine *Black Book
of Polish Censorship*
that named blacklisted
figures in 1970s Poland.
Ford committed suicide
in Florida in 1980.

Shooting from the ruins

The Second World War destroyed the strong Jewish vein
in Polish filmmaking, and, similarly, the wider Polish film
industry was left in ruins. With the Communists now
in power, Film Polski, a state-controlled body, began to
rebuild the movie-making infrastructure. Initially, Film
Polski was led by Aleksander Ford (born Mosze Lifszyc),
previously a film propagandist in wartime Soviet Union.
He rejuvenated film production and directed various
state-sponsored features himself, such as Poland's first
post-war colour picture, *Piątka z ulicy Barskiej* (*Five Boys
from Barska Street*) (1954), about a group of boys trying
to survive in demolished Warsaw, which found its way to
the Cannes Film Festival.

Something special in Łódź

On 8th March 1948, theatre director Leon Schiller (see
section 4.2.3) established a Film School in Łódź. The city
was chosen because, unlike Warsaw, it had a functioning
film production studio and access to decent equipment.
The school became the breeding ground for a new
generation of excellent Polish filmmakers. Initially the
directors, cinematographers and actors worked within the
creative confines of Socialist Realism (see section 1.2.3),
but after Stalin's death in 1953 found they could pursue
their craft with more autonomy – film became one of the
few areas of cultural life in which artistic expression was
allowed. A remarkably fecund period of Polish cinema
followed. The Łódź alumni looked back to Poland's
wartime struggle for material, but also, with remarkable
skill, made implicit their discomfort with the country's
post-war regime.

Wajda and his Wartime Trilogy

The first significant graduate of the Łódź Film School was
Andrzej Wajda. Apprenticed to Aleksander Ford at Film
Polski, he released his first feature film in 1955. *Pokolenie*
(*A Generation*) was set in a poor district of Nazi-occupied
Warsaw and portrayed Stach and Jasio, two young men

148

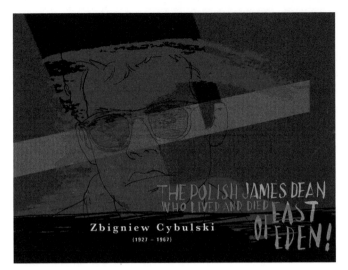

THE POLISH JAMES DEAN
WHO LIVED AND DIED EAST OF EDEN!

Zbigniew Cybulski
(1927 – 1967)

drawn into the Communist resistance. Filmed amid the post-war rubble and acted with moody understatement, *Pokolenie* was revelatory. The film's underlying tension, fired by the individual's struggle under a repressive political and social order, would resonate in Wajda's future work. He followed *Pokolenie* with two more outstanding films to complete what became known as his Wartime Trilogy. Each had its cast of uncompromising, desperate young men, and each dealt with Poland's multilayered wartime resistance from a different angle. *Kanał* (*Canal*) (1956) followed a troupe of Home Army fighters in the tragic final days of the 1944 Warsaw Uprising, whilst *Popiół i diament* (*Ashes and Diamonds*) (1958) switched attention to the anti-Communist resistance fighting in Poland at the war's end. Wajda was already a master at symbolism, and his talent for allegory – regularly referencing Poland's post-war occupation – would grow over the coming decades.

Poster boy

Quiffed and insouciant, Zbigniew Cybulski has often been called the Polish James Dean. He spent much of his early career in theatre, but got his big film break playing the lead in Aleksander Ford's *Eighth Day of the Week*. In Wajda's *Ashes and Diamonds*, his career hit its peak, playing Maciek, a Home Army soldier asked to assassinate a Communist bigwig. He starred in various films throughout the 1960s, some of them foreign, but never revisited his early success. Cybulski died in 1967, aged 39. He was running for a late night train at Wrocław Station when he apparently fell beneath the wheels. Some suggested it might have been suicide. His death inspired Wajda to make *Wszystko na sprzedaż* (*Everything For Sale*) (1968), a poorly received 'film within a film'

Glowing embers

In 2010, 52 years after its first release, *Ashes and Diamonds* was ranked number 38 in *Empire Magazine's* 100 Best Films of World Cinema.

5.1.3 A golden age: the Polish Film School
and Cinema of Moral Concern

The Polish Film School

Where Wajda led, a glut of young and exciting filmmakers
followed. The success of his Wartime Trilogy, not least at
Cannes, had thrown the international spotlight on Polish
cinema and, appreciating the kudos, Film Polski allowed
its production units and young directors a certain degree
of freedom. They formed a loose Polish Film School,
influenced by the Italian Neorealists and keen to portray
the individual's struggle against authority. Poland's recent
wartime experience was a recurrent theme. Despite their
relative freedom, filmmakers still operated within the
bounds of censorship, and most would shoot the majority
of their films in exile having first established a reputation
in Poland.

Six important directors from the Polish Film School

Andrzej Munk. Where Wajda portrayed romantic struggle,
Munk made his characters more ambiguous. He made
Eroica (*Heroism*) (1957), an 'anti-heroic' film of two halves:
the first featuring a soldier in the 1944 fight for Warsaw,
and the second about the exploits of a Polish POW. Munk
died in a car crash in 1961, midway through production
on *Pasażerka* (*Passenger*) (1963), in which an Auschwitz
survivor encounters a camp guard after the war.

Kazimierz Kutz. A director who began with the Realist
war film *Krzyż Walecznych* (*Cross of Valour*) (1959), and
went on to make films exploring the individual's psyche in
wartime, often featuring his native Silesia, before moving
into theatre direction, lecturing and politics, culminating in
his election to the Polish Senate in 1997.

Jerzy Kawalerowicz. Kawalerowicz impressed with a
trilogy of war films in the late 1950s but was celebrated
primarily for *Matka Joanna od aniołów* (*Mother Joan of
the Angels*) (1961), ostensibly about demonic possession
in a 17th century convent, but with references to a
domineering authority (from Church and State) that few in
Poland could misinterpret. A director with a remarkably

1. Identity: the   2. Literature   3. Art, architecture   4. Music, theatre,   **5. Cinema**   6. Media and   7. Food and drink   8. Living culture:
foundations   and philosophy   and design   and comedy   **and fashion**   communications   the state of
of Polish culture   modern Poland

diverse repertoire – he had no recurrent theme – Kawalerowicz went on to film versions of historic Polish novels, including Bolesław Prus' *Faraon* (*Pharaoh*) (1966) and Henryk Sienkiewicz' *Quo Vadis* (2001).

Roman Polanski. Polanski played one of the youths in Wajda's *A Generation*, but his long, distinguished career has been defined by directing. His debut, *Nóż w wodzie* (*Knife in the Water*) (1962), a psychological drama about a married couple who give a young hitchhiker a lift, established his reputation and angered the authorities with its references to consumerism. Polanski duly fled Poland and began making English-language films. His broad, internationally lauded repertoire finds consistency in disturbed protagonists, studied in detail, their malevolence or suffering carefully dissected.

Jerzy Skolimowski. Skolimowski's first notable contribution to Polish cinema was as co-author of Polanski's *Knife in the Water*, after which he spent two decades compiling six semi-autobiographical movies. The third, *Ręce do góry* (*Hands Up!*) (1967), in which the director himself played his own alter ego, was banned for its satire on Polish society. Skolimowski continued making reflective, philosophical films in exile; *The Lightship* (1984), starring Robert Duvall, was the big success.

Krzysztof Zanussi. An auteur director whose first feature, *Struktura kryształu* (*The Structure of Crystal*) (1969), established a pattern for films that explored the complex moral dilemmas of their protagonists. *Życie rodzinne* (*Family Life*) (1971) cemented Zanussi's reputation, and later works such as *Barwy ochronne* (*Camouflage*) (1976) helped kick-start the Cinema of Moral Concern (see more page 152).

Three baptisms of fire

Andrzej Munk. Aged 18 when war broke out, Munk, of Jewish descent, assumed a false name when the Nazis invaded. In 1944 he fought in the Warsaw Uprising, the failed insurrection featured in the outstanding *Heroism*.

Roman Polanski. The Polanskis were put in the Kraków Ghetto when Roman was six. His father was sent to Mauthausen concentration camp but survived. His mother died in Auschwitz. Polanski fled the ghetto in 1943 and assumed the identity of a Roman Catholic boy, Romek Wilk, before living feral in the countryside. The horrors Polanski witnessed have informed his work.

Jerzy Skolimowski. He was apparently rescued from a bombed-out house in Warsaw as a small child. Skolimowski's father, a member of the Polish resistance, was executed by the Nazis, whilst his mother hid a Jewish family in their home.

The devil has all the best tunes, films, books, plays, operas…

The story in Jerzy Kawalerowicz's *Mother Joan of the Angels* was inspired by events in the French town of Loudin in 1634. Nuns at the town's Ursuline convent became infatuated with Urbain Grandier, a philandering Catholic priest. When he turned down their offer of a permanent job at the convent, Sister Jeanne accused him of using sorcery to seduce and demonically possess the nuns. Cardinal Richelieu took the opportunity to convict the priest of witchcraft and had him burned at the stake. Kawalerowicz' film explores what happened in the years after his death; Aldous Huxley (book), John Whiting (play), Krzysztof Penderecki (opera) and Ken Russell (film) all used the same story as inspiration for works in the 20th century.

Five great English-language films by Polanski

Rosemary's Baby (1968). Genuinely disturbing film about a young pregnant woman (Mia Farrow) and her creepy neighbours' plans for the child. Bagged a brace of Oscars.

Chinatown (1974). Neo-noir starring Jack Nicholson as the private eye who uncovers corruption and murder in 1930s Los Angeles. Nominated for 11 Oscars.

Tess (1979). Shot in exile in France, Polanski's take on the Thomas Hardy classic won three Academy Awards.

The Pianist (2001). Polanski's first film about the Holocaust won the Palme d'Or at Cannes, two César awards in France and the 2002 Oscar for Best Director.

The Ghost Writer (2010). Ewan McGregor starred in the adaptation of Robert Harris' political thriller. Germany stood in for Martha's Vineyard thanks to Polanski's ongoing fugitive status in the USA.

Moral victories: film in the 1970s

Graduates of the Łódź Film School continued making important films throughout the 1970s. Wajda remained the leading light, chipping away at the status quo with films that explored Polish society. In 1977 he made *Człowiek z marmaru* (*Man of Marble*), in which a documentary maker investigates the disappearance of a heroic 'Stakhanovite' worker, as championed in the Stalinist era. To many, the inference was clear – the working classes had been abandoned by the state. *Man of Marble* helped initiate the informal Cinema of Moral Concern (or Anxiety), as the subsequent slew of documentary-inspired films became known. For both filmmakers and audiences, the 'enemy' was easily identifiable; as such, it didn't need naming directly but could still be critiqued. Even so, the movement, such as it was, wasn't overtly political, keen instead to explore the wider moral health of Polish life and history. Two directors in particular emerged from the Cinema of Moral Concern to become key figures in Polish film:

Agnieszka Holland. Holland worked as an assistant to Wajda for years before finding her own directorial feet with *Aktorzy prowincjonalni* (*Provincial Actors*) (1978). Ostensibly, the film was about a small-town theatre production, but the themes of claustrophobia and tension without release resonated with the Poles' wider life-experience. The film won the International Critics Prize in Cannes. Most of Holland's subsequent films, including the Oscar-nominated *Europa Europa* (1991), were made outside Poland.

Krzysztof Kieślowski. A director who cut his teeth making documentaries about life under the Communists, and duly found his work heavily censored. Kieślowski made the Cinema for Moral Concern's signature piece, *Amator* (*Camera Buff*) (1979), the story of a factory

Whilst most of the young directors associated with the Polish Film School made obliquely political movies, another filmmaker, Wojciech Has, was more individualistic, shooting psychological dramas or creating labyrinthine worlds and dreamscapes reminiscent of the Surrealist painters. *Rękopis znaleziony w Saragossie* (*The Saragossa Manuscript*) (1964)), a three-hour adaptation of Jan Potocki's novel (see section 2.1.3), was perhaps his most lauded film.

Life on the run

Since 1978 Roman Polanski has been making his films in Europe. In the USA he is wanted as a fugitive, having skipped the country on the day he was due in court to face charges of having sexual relations with a 13-year-old girl, Samantha Geimer (Polanski had already pleaded guilty and was facing a possible life sentence). When the director won an Oscar in 2002 for *The Pianist*, actor Harrison Ford collected the award on his behalf.

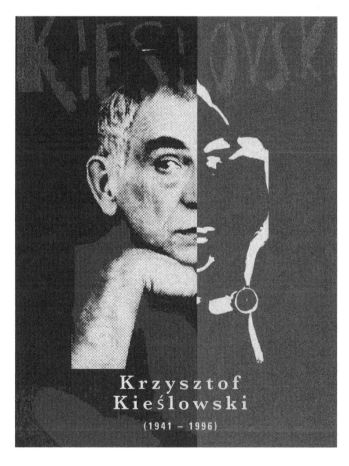

Krzysztof Kieślowski
(1941 – 1996)

worker turned amateur cameraman who finds his creative expression limited by the authorities. A subsequent work, *Przypadek* (*Blind Chance*) (1981) was banned. In later years, Kieślowski would enjoy international success with, amongst other things, *Dekalog* (1989), an epic TV series that updated the Ten Commandments for modern-day Poland.

The curtain comes down

The Cinema for Moral Concern ended in 1981, and brought Poland's anomalously expressive and fruitful post-war cinematic experience to an end with it. The imposition of martial law in December 1981 included a clampdown on film; any politically orientated material was censored and its producers stopped from working. Wajda made one of the last great Polish films of the period – *Człowiek z żelaza* (*Man of Iron*) (1981). The film is set in the Gdańsk Shipyard, where the young protagonist leads a strike against the authorities, mirroring the real events of the time (see section 1.2.3). *Man of Iron* won the Palme d'Or at Cannes but was banned in Poland when martial law was declared. With Wajda, Skolimowski, Polanski, Holland, Kieślowski and many others fleeing Poland to work in exile (where they continued to make significant films), and with those that remained banned, tarnished by association with the state or limited to 'populist' comedies, audience figures dropped and Polish cinema ended the Communist years at a limp.

154

| 1. Identity: the foundations of Polish culture | 2. Literature and philosophy | 3. Art, architecture and design | 4. Music, theatre and comedy | **5. Cinema and fashion** | 6. Media and communications | 7. Food and drink | 8. Living culture: the state of modern Poland |

5.1.4 The new auteurs: modern Polish cinema

The realities of freedom

Polish cinema was freed from censorship when the Communists were voted out of power in 1989. Correspondingly, it also had to become more self-sufficient; the state funding of previous decades was reduced. As a result, bona fide homegrown cinema rather struggled through the final decade of the 20th century. Lightweight comedies and historical epics provided much of the content, whilst 'serious' cinema came from the established directors like Holland, Kieślowski and Polanski who were making films with foreign money. Kieślowski, perhaps, stood above the crowd, with a trilogy of films, *Trois Couleurs* (*Three Colours*) (1993-4) – *Bleu, Blanc and Rouge* – that were French-funded and themed, but made with Polish expertise, in particular scriptwriter Krzysztof Piesiewicz. The director died in the midst of open-heart surgery soon after the trilogy was made.

Modern movies and moviegoers

The film industry in Poland has been resurgent in the 21st century. It may not quite have the international reach of old, but for native audiences there has been much to savour. Variety has been key, with comedies, thrillers, historical epics, documentaries and art house films all a part of the scene. A new generation of directors, the likes of Wojciech Smarzowski (*Wesele* (*The Wedding*) (2004)), Urszula Urbaniak (*Torowisko* (*The Junction* (1999)), Dariusz Gajewski (*Lekcje pana Kuki* (*Mr Kuka's Advice*) (2007)) and Małgorzata Szumowska (*33 sceny z życia* (*33 Scenes from Life*) (2008)), have made films about transition and life in newly democratised Poland. Others, including the directors who helped Polish cinema punch above its weight for decades, have reverted to the wartime themes of the Polish School, notably Wajda,

Going, going, going, going... gong
Four of Andrzej Wajda's films have been nominated for the Best Foreign Language Film Oscar but the Director's sole Academy gong was actually an honorary award, given in 2000 in recognition of his contribution to world cinema.

155

1. Identity: the foundations of Polish culture 2. Literature and philosophy 3. Art, architecture and design 4. Music, theatre, and comedy **5. Cinema and fashion** 6. Media and communications 7. Food and drink 8. Living culture: the state of modern Poland

Given the bird

The Polskie Nagrody
Filmowe Orly, the Polish
Film Awards, or 'Eagles',
have been given out
once a year since 1999.
Winners receive the
statuette of a white
eagle, as designed
by sculptor Adam
Fedorowicz. The biggest
winners in the awards'
short history have been
Polanski's *The Pianist*
(2002) and *Rewers*
(*The Reverse*) (2009), a
dark comedy by Borys
Lankosz set in Stalin-era
Warsaw. Both received
eight Eagles.

Polanski and Holland, respectively in *Katyń* (2007) (a popular success some 54 years after Wajda's first feature), *The Pianist* (2002) and *In Darkness* (2011).

Today, Poland, like much of Europe, laps up the latest offerings from the Hollywood studios. However, the last decade has also witnessed a sharp rise in the number of filmgoers watching Polish movies. Around one in eight films released in Poland is now Polish. The country's accession into the EU has helped; the film industry in Poland now benefits from MEDIA funding, whilst foreign filmmakers also appear keen to shoot there.

A taste of contemporary Polish cinema: ten films

Polish film fest

Poland's premier film
festival is held each
May in Gdynia, and is
called, not unreasonably,
Festiwal Polskich Filmów
Fabularnych w Gdyni
(the Festival of Polish
Feature Films in Gdynia).
The best film receives
The Golden Lion award.
Jerzy Hoffman won in
the first year, 1974, with
Potop (*The Deluge*), an
adaptation of Henryk
Sienkiewicz' famous
novel (see section 2.1.4).
Further afield, both
Seattle and Hollywood
host an annual Polish
film festival.

Życie jako śmiertelna choroba przenoszona drogą płciową (*Life as a Fatal Sexually Transmitted Disease*) (2000) Krzysztof Zanussi. Focusing on the final weeks of a doctor's life, and made by a much-lauded director and producer.

Katedra (*The Cathedral*) (2002) Tomasz Bagiński. Short, silent science-fiction film nominated for an Oscar.

Wesele (*The* Wedding) (2004) Wojciech Smarzowski. Hugely popular black comedy centred on the less-than-smooth nuptials of Kate and Janusz.

1. Identity: the   2. Literature   3. Art, architecture   4. Music, theatre,   **5. Cinema**   6. Media and   7. Food and drink   8. Living culture:
foundations   and philosophy   and design   and comedy   **and fashion**   communications   the state of
of Polish culture   modern Poland

Katyń (2007) Andrzej Wajda. Wajda's dramatisation of the mass execution of Polish officers by Soviet forces in 1940 was a commercial and critical success.

Wszyscy jesteśmy Chrystusami (*We are all Christs*) (2007) Marek Koterski. In which the Miauczyńskis face up to alcoholism and its impact on family life. Won Best Film at the Polish Film Awards.

Sztuczki (*Tricks*) (2007) Andrzej Jakimowski. Stefek, a six-year-old boy, uses all kinds of 'tricks' to get closer to a father that doesn't even know he has a son.

Cztery noce z Anna (*Four Nights with Anna*) (2008) Jerzy Skolimowski. One of the old directorial guard tells the story of a mortuary worker obsessed with Anna.

33 sceny z życia (*33 Scenes from Life*) (2008) Małgorzata Szumowska. The bleak story of an artist, Julia, confronted by a series of family crises.

Róża (2011) Wojciech Smarzowski. Love and anguish, explored in the midst of Poland's wartime identity crisis.

W ciemności (*In Darkness*) (2011) Agnieszka Holland. Inspired by the true story of Jews hidden in the sewers of Nazi-occupied Lwów. Oscar nominated.

Sharp shooters

Polish cinematographers have made a name for themselves in Hollywood. Janusz Kaminski has been Director of Photography on every single Steven Spielberg film since *Schindler's List* (1993), whilst Sławomir Idziak has worked on films such as *Black Hawk Down* (2001) and *Harry Potter and the Order of the Phoenix* (2007).

Five important Polish animators

Jan Lenica. A graphic designer who also made animated films, such as *Ubu et la grande gidouille* (1979), produced in exile in France.

Walerian Borowczyk. Another director who spent most of his career in France, making acclaimed animated features like *Théâtre de Monsieur & Madame Kabal* (1967), before moving over to live action films.

Jerzy Kucia. The director of several acclaimed, avant-garde animated shorts, including *Strojenie instrumentów* (*Tuning the Instruments*) (2000).

Piotr Dumała. Has used 'destructive animation', in which one image is erased and replaced by the next, for short films based on novels by Franz Kafka and Fyodor Dostoyevsky.

Zbigniew Rybczynski. Won a Best Animated Short Oscar for *Tango* (1983), in which the action in one room is built up piece by piece, rather like a visual fugue.

5.2 Fashion

In a country where, until relatively recently, wearing the wrong clothes could result in imprisonment, it is perhaps unsurprising that Poland doesn't have an international reputation for fashion. However, look to the regional traditions, to the nation's history and to an emerging pack of young designers and a fascinating sartorial story takes shape.

The Bikini Boys

In the early1950s, young Polish men developed an equivalent to the Teddy Boy look popular in the West. The wearers were known as Bikiniarze, 'Bikini Boys', not for their choice of a two-piece swimsuit, but because, like the more famous women's bikini, they emerged in the era of hydrogen bomb testing in the Pacific Ocean. The Bikiniarze were demonised as degenerate by the state, and often detained and beaten.

Dressing to impress: Sarmatian style

Historically, Poland enjoyed its finest fashion hour during the Rzeczpospolita (see section 1.2.2), in the centuries when it was the dominant power in central Europe. The Polish-Lithuanian nobility cultivated a particular form of dress to reinforce their delusions of a grand Sarmatian heritage. Aristocratic men wore an Ottoman-inspired robe, the *kontusz*, held in place by

an ornately decorated and tasselled sash. A *kołpak* (fur-brimmed hat), knee-high leather boots, *szabla* (ceremonial saber) and flamboyant moustache completed the ensemble. The women, similarly, wore a long and flowing *kontusz*, often with fur trim, and a hat that resembled a turban with feathers attached. In the subsequent centuries, during which Poland lost much of its power and territory, the upper reaches of society fell in step with whatever style was doing the rounds of Europe.

The sartorial straitjacket: dressing for communism

The privation of life under Communist rule stunted fashion in Poland. Money wasn't available for clothes that stepped outside the utilitarian state-sanctioned norm, and the tight controls on production ensured that the flamboyance of Western fashion in the 1960s and '70s largely passed Poland by. Certain concessions were made – Poland began producing its own denim jeans in 1975 – but the association of colourful, progressive fashion with the West made it off-limits. Inevitably, however, a black market developed. Younger Poles made their own clothes, emulating the styles that filtered through from the USA and UK, using their clothes as a means of self-expression. Gradually, the authorities loosened the reins; although anyone wearing colourful or unconventional clothing remained a target for suspicion right through to the punk outfits of the late 1970s and early '80s.

Colour coded: Polish folk costumes

Poland's traditional folk costumes, of which there are hundreds, follow a common formula. Detailed, highly coloured embroidery is widely used. Women usually sport ankle boots, a full and colourful skirt, an apron and an embroidered or sequinned waistcoat. Hair is plaited and woven with ribbons and flowers. For Polish men, typical folk outfits swap the women's skirt for colourful trousers tucked into boots. A hat, often a black boater with a coloured ribbon, completes the outfit. Today, such costumes are only worn on special occasions – at festivals, on national holidays and at suitable weddings. Each region, or even town, has its own variation: the detailing on the embroidery may be different, the style of the hat may vary, or boots will be exchanged for shoes. In rural areas, older women may still wear a more humdrum 'traditional dress', consisting of simple headscarf and apron.

From catwalk to high street

Today, Poles dress similarly to most Westerners. An American look predominates – leather jackets, jeans and t-shirts – and the high street clothes stores are the same as those found throughout Europe. The country

Three regional costumes

Podhale. The male highlanders of Podhale wear white woollen trousers and shirts, sheepskin waistcoats and a flat black hat adorned with seashells. The women opt for floral skirts and embroidered vests. Brown, moccasin-style *kierpce* shoes are worn by both.

Poznań. In certain villages around Poznań, the Bambrzy Poles, descended in part from Germans, wear lacy white aprons, black shoes, plain-coloured blouses and a headdress made from flowers.

Kraków. Conjure an image of Poland's national costume and it probably looks something like the traditional dress worn around Kraków: embroidered waistcoats or bodices, aprons and hats adorned with peacock feathers.

Modern Fashion Designer:
Kamila Gawronska-Kasperska

FROM HER **METROPOLIS No 3** COLLECTION

looks to the fashion capitals of Paris, London and New York for the latest trends, but also has its own fashion week, Fashion Philosophy, held in Łódź, home city of the Polish textile industry. The leading designer at the show is awarded the Golden Thread, the most prestigious prize in Polish fashion. In Kraków, the renowned School of Art and Fashion Design has made the city a hub for emergent designers (and Kraków has been named as one of the world's top 25 cities for fashion). Each year the school holds the highly respected Kraków Fashion Awards.

Six important Polish fashion designers

Barbara Hulanicki. Born in pre-war Warsaw, Hulanicki is probably Poland's most famous fashion export. After studying at the Brighton School of Art, she sold her clothes through a small mail-order company, and by 1964 was ready to open her first store, Biba, in Kensington, London. Hulanicki's fabric choices, risqué mini skirts and the quick turnover of affordable designs made Biba synonymous with the swinging '60s. More recently, her Biba-inspired line for British store Topshop sold out in minutes.

Kamila Gawrońska-Kasperska. An avant-garde designer known for structural, futuristic collections, often in monochrome, such as the Metropolis collection inspired by Fritz Lang's 1927 film.

Ewa Minge. Hailed as 'the Polish Donatella Versace', Minge has achieved international acclaim, finding a particularly fervid following in New York. The Szczecinek-born designer has been responsible for styling Miss Poland and Elite Model Look contestants, as well as Poland's former First Lady, Jolanta Kwaśniewska.

Krystof Strozyna. Burst onto the scene in 2007 with his Central Saint Martins graduate collection, taking second place in the Harrods Design Award. Renowned for a 'perfectly fitted, graphic cut dress', Strozyna's A-list fans include Nicole Scherzinger and Natalia Vodianova.

Dawid Tomaszewski. Gdańsk-born Tomaszewski has stayed true to his Polish roots by collaborating with some of Poland's most eminent creatives (notably, jazz pianist Paweł Kaczmarczyk and artist Michal Martychowiec). Tomaszewski also designed for Reebok and Comme des Garçons before setting up his own label.

Gosia Baczyńska. Baczyńska trained in London but opened her studio and first store in Warsaw. Known for a feminine style, she won popularity and awards with a limited collection, Le Carrousel, for the Polish clothing company Reserved.

Three Polish models

Anja Rubik. Born in Częstochowa in 1985, Rubik is arguably Poland's 'supermodel', having worked for everyone from Gucci to Victoria's Secret and H&M.

Anna Jagodzińska. One of the most in-demand Polish models; has appeared on the cover of *Vogue* in most of its national variants.

Monika Jagaciak. Discovered at an open casting in a Poznań shopping centre, at the age of 13 she won a campaign with Hermes; but was banned from Australian Fashion Week for being too young a year later.

6 Media and communications

6.1 Media

Having been carefully controlled by the state for much of the 20th century, Poland's unrestrained and partly deregulated media is enjoying its newfound freedom, even if it is often the freedom to simply print gossip and broadcast soaps.

1. Identity: the foundations of Polish culture

2. Literature and philosophy

3. Art, architecture and design

4. Music, theatre and comedy

5. Cinema and fashion

6. Media and communications

7 Food and drink

8. Living culture: the state of modern Poland

Freedom of the press...at last

The Polish press has endured a long and troubled history. Ever since the first newspaper appeared in the 17th century, print media has been subject to extensive periods of censorship. The Russians, Prussians, Austrians, Germans and Soviets all, at various times, controlled and limited its scope. How refreshing then to be in a period of freedom for the press today, as enshrined by law in the republic's young constitution. This freedom, coupled with the privatisation of previously state-owned publications (with a high level of foreign investment) and the appearance of several new periodicals, finds Poland producing some 5,000 regular print media titles. Over 300 of these are newspapers, the vast majority of which are regional or local. Alas, the picture isn't entirely rosy: circulation figures show a downward trend and only 30 per cent of Poles regularly read a paper.

The Polish press: key dates

1661 The first Polish newspaper *Merkuriusz Polski*, much of it written in Latin, was printed in Krakow under the sponsorship of Jan II Kazimierz Waza's royal court. It lasted for seven months and 41 issues.

1765 *Monitor*, a highly respected weekly newspaper modelled on the English *Spectator*, was published. For 20 years, *Monitor* expressed the reforming ideals of the Enlightenment.

1945 Główny Urząd Kontroli Prasy, Publikacji i Widowisk (the Central Office of Control of the Press, Publications and Performances) was created in Warsaw. The body would oversee the scrutiny of almost every word printed during the Communist years.

1984 The struggling regime introduced the 1984 Press Law, going some way towards guaranteeing freedom of expression, access to information and media rights.

1989 *Gazeta Wyborcza* was printed, becoming the first official newspaper published outside the control of the Communist government.

1990 Parliament modified the 1984 Press Law, ending censorship of the press.

The big five dailies

Fakt

Launched in 2003 by German media company Axel Springer, *Fakt* is the biggest selling Polish daily (circulation approx 600,000). With a politically central stance, the paper pursues a relatively lowbrow, sensationalist style that targets a blue-collar readership.

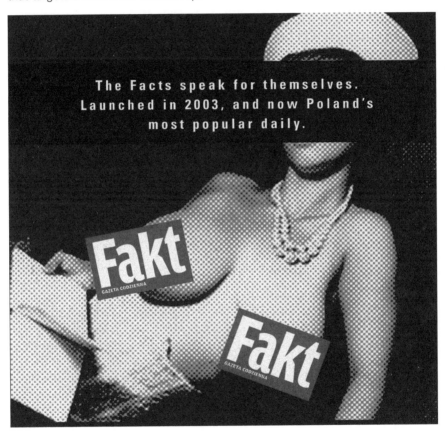

The Facts speak for themselves. Launched in 2003, and now Poland's most popular daily.

169

1 Identity: the foundations of Polish culture   2 Literature and philosophy   3 Art, architecture and design   4 Music, theatre, and comedy   5 Cinema and fashion   **6. Media and communications**   7 Food and drink   8 Living culture: the state of modern Poland

Paper cuts

In 1977 Tomasz Strzyżewski, a censor in Kraków, smuggled classified documents published in *The Black Book of Polish Censorship (Czarna ksiega cenzury PRL)* out of Poland. They revealed the extent of the Communist regime's ludicrous obsession with the control of information, and the retribution taken on 'offenders'. A newspaper that published a few stray words on political or social affairs, for example, would find its paper provision drastically reduced, so that fewer people could read the next issue.

Gazeta Wyborcza

Founded in 1989 as the mouthpiece of the Solidarity movement, *Gazeta Wyborcza* has become the most influential quality Polish newspaper (circulation approx 420,000). The paper holds liberal-left views, and, along with *Rzeczpospolita* (see below), is the newspaper of choice for the educated Pole. Owned by Polish company, Agora.

Metro

Another Agora title, *Metro* is a free daily distributed in 18 Polish cities (circulation approx 400,000). Since 2008, *Metro* has remodelled itself as a paper focusing on the interests of younger people, with sections devoted to education, recruitment, etc.

Super Express

Owned by Polish company MediaExpress, *Super Express* started life in 1991 as a 'quality', opinion-forming newspaper, but reinvented itself as a tabloid (in style) in order to compete with *Fakt*. The stance is populist with a hint of nationalism (circulation approx 300,000).

Rzeczpospolita

Founded in 1920 with connections to the Catholic Church, *Rzeczpospolita* became the official newspaper of the government before being rendered obsolete in 1950 by *Trybuna Ludu*, the Communist Party's paper. In 1982 it was revived, and finally became independent in 1991. A 'quality' paper, *Rzeczpospolita* sits on the centre-right of the political spectrum (circulation approx 200,000).

Regional and sports press

In addition to the nationals, Poland harbours several regional and local newspapers. The best respected of these include *Gazeta Krakowska*, a daily paper in Kraków launched in 1949, and *Gazeta Olsztyńska*, based in Olsztyn and first published in 1886. The country's only daily sports newspaper, *Przegląd Sportowy* (circulation approx 100,000), first printed in 1921, is well known for its annual Sports Personality of the Year award. A trio of English language journals, the *Kraków Post*, a monthly, and *The Warsaw Voice* and *New Poland Express* (online), both issued weekly, also reach a wide audience.

News, fashion and gossip: Polish magazines
Poland has hundreds of weekly and monthly magazines, catering for almost every conceivable taste, with publications concerning cars (such as *Auto Świat*), fashion (*Avanti*), television (*Tele Tydzień*) and cookery (*Przyślij Przepis*). The most popular titles include:

Polityka
Founded in 1957, the liberal-left leaning *Polityka* is the biggest selling quality news magazine in Poland (circulation approx 200,000). The closest competitors are the centrist *Wprost*, first published in 1982, and the glossy Polish edition of *Newsweek*.

Claudia
A monthly women's magazine offering information and advice on fashion, cosmetics, interior design, etc. since 1991, *Claudia* boasts a huge readership (circulation approx 500,000). Similar publications include *Chwila dla Ciebie*, and *Twój Styl*, whose 300,000 readers can vote for their Style Woman of the Year.

Party - Życie Gwiazd!
The Poles love their celebrity gossip, and the pages of big selling bi-weekly *Party - Życie Gwiazd!* (or 'Party – Life of the Stars!') are awash with the stuff (circulation approx 500,000). *Show* is a similar affair, and sells a comparable number of copies.

1. Identity: the
foundations ·
of Polish culture

2. Literature
and philosophy

3. Art, architecture
and design

4. Music, theatre,
and comedy

5. Cinema
and fashion

**6. Media and
communications**

7. Food and drink

8. Living culture:
the state of
modern Poland

6.1.2 Viewing habits: television

Reality check: four talent shows

Mam talent! The title translates, without hint of irony, as 'I've Got Talent!'. It's Poland's version of the *XXX's Got Talent* franchise, and pulls in around five million viewers a week.

X Factor. You know the drill. A talent show aired on TVN, in which the winner receives 100,000 zł and a recording contract with Sony Music.

Top Model. Zostań modelką. Another TVN talent show, this one hosted by Polish-born supermodel Joanna Krupa. Contestants fight it out for a modelling contract with the Next agency.

Taniec z gwiazdami. A ballroom dancing contest, broadcast by TVN. Attracts more than seven million viewers on a Sunday evening.

Channelling the regime

In the bad old days, Polish television was an instrument of state propaganda, frequently used to disseminate misinformation or for the aggrandisement of the Communist regime. When Pope John Paul II visited his homeland in June 1979, for example, television reports maintained that few bothered to go and hear him give mass; but every Pole knew that he had addressed hundreds of thousands of people. The phrase 'he lies like TV' duly became commonplace amongst dissidents in the 1970s.

In the years of broadcasting freedom since 1989, television has become an important facet of Polish culture, occupying four hours of the average Pole's day. The annual TV licence costs 188.30 zł; the fee split 60/40 between the public television and radio broadcasting bodies. However, licence evasion is widespread, with an estimated 45 per cent of households dodging the annual fee, leading to proposals that the public broadcasters be funded directly from the state purse.

The big TV channels

Polish television is dominated by the four largest free-to-air channels – TVP1, TVP2, TVN and Polsat – which gobble up more than 60 per cent of audience share. Each has a similar menu, delivering a diet of news and general entertainment (soaps, dramas and comedies, many of them dubbed from English). TVP1 and TVP2 are the main channels of Telewizja Polska (TVP), Poland's public broadcasting corporation, which launched in 1952. Other TVP output includes TVP Info (which hosts regional channels), TVP Polonia (for Poles abroad) and special interest channels on history, culture, etc. available on satellite and cable.

TVN, launched in 1997, and Polsat, established in 1992, are the leading free-to-air commercial channels. Both also offer pay-TV channels for films, sport, etc. Aside from its free-to-air channels, Poland also has myriad cable, satellite and IPTV (internet TV) options, available via various paid-for packages. Such pay-TV channels are hugely popular – approx ten million households subscribe.

Judgement Day for Nergal

There's plenty to complain about when it comes to TV talent shows: the bullying, the commerciality and the ephemeral nature of any subsequent success for its contestants. But when Bishop Wiesław Mering raised concerns about *Najlepszy głos* (*The Voice of Poland*), a singing contest broadcast weekly on TVP, none of the issues above featured. His objection was that one of the judges, Adam Darski, aka 'Nergal', was what he called a 'Satanist'. The bishop felt that the lead singer of death metal group Behemoth, who ripped up a Bible on stage in 2007, wasn't fit and proper for a place on the judging panel of such a high profile primetime programme.

What's on the box?
Five popular shows

Klan. Poland's longest-running soap opera first aired in 1997 on TVP1. It charts the ups and downs of the fictional Lubicz family from Warsaw, five days a week.

M jak miłość. The most popular Polish television drama, the title of which translates as 'L for Love', attracts 12 million viewers twice a week on TVP2, all tuning in for the latest dramas of the Mostowiak family.

Plebania. Another popular TVP1 soap, this one concerning life in the fictional village of Tulczyn. Plebania translates as 'The Parish'.

Na dobre i na złe. A medical drama running on TVP2 since 1999, revolving around the lives of doctors and patients in a Polish hospital. Title translates as 'For Better or Worse'.

Ranczo. TVP1 comedy series, 'The Ranch', set in the small fictional town of Wilkowyje.

What are the Poles watching?

Polish television has its share of respected current affairs programmes. *Wiadomości* is the main news program on TVP1, broadcast daily at 7.30pm (a traditional slot for the news in Poland) and watched by an average of 4.3 million Poles. Talk shows also get reasonable viewing figures; they vary from the serious – *Tomasz Lis na żywo* – to the satirical – *Szymon Majewski* Show and *Kuba Wojewódzki* (with a host of the same name). However, current affairs programmes don't dominate the viewing figures. Soaps are far more popular and, it seems, the Poles have also fallen under the spell of reality TV. The tried and tested reality and talent show formats of other nations abound here too, littering the schedules.

Glued to the wireless

The Poles have enjoyed a lengthy love affair with their radios. In the years of Soviet control, the wireless offered a certain escapism, albeit one closely monitored by the state. With reliable information in short supply, many listened in secret to Radio Free Europe, a station broadcast by the CIA, and which

the Polish government did its best to jam. Today, Poland has more than 200 radio stations to choose from. On average, Poles tune in for 4.7 hours a day – significantly longer than elsewhere in Europe. The annual TV licence (see section 6.1.2) covers radio use, although a radio-only licence is also available for 58.75 zł per year.

The four nationwide public stations

Jedynka (1). For news, current affairs and light entertainment.

Dwójka (2). Classical music and cultural programmes.

Trójka (3). A mix of jazz and rock music.

Czwórka (4). An educational channel.

Public and commercial

Polskie Radio is Poland's public radio network, funded in part by its share of the TV licence fee. It was founded in 1925 and controlled by Polskie Radio i Telewizja (Polish Radio and Television), which was split into its two constituent parts in 1992. Polskie Radio operates the country's four main nationwide channels, 17 regional radio stations and a handful of internet-only channels that carry parliamentary debates and foreign language broadcasts. Commercial radio, which emerged with Poland's transition to democracy, has become the dominant player in the market, accounting for three out of every four listeners.

Making waves

The most controversial radio station in Poland is Radio Maryja, founded in Toruń in 1991 by Father Tadeusz Rydzyk. It's a Roman Catholic station with a predominantly elderly and rural listenership of around 1.2 million a day. The content could often be described as right-wing extremism, and has drawn criticism from all sides – including the Vatican – for its anti-Semitic, homophobic, xenophobic, anti-abortion, anti-European Union and pro-death penalty stance – which its founder likes to call 'patriotism'.

Underground via London

The SWIT radio station is fondly remembered in Poland. It provided vital and up-to-date news and information during the German occupation in the Second World War. The Nazis searched high and low for the illicit station without success – it was actually broadcasting from London, relaying information covertly supplied by the Polish Underground

Matysiakowie. A radio soap set around the fictional (titular) family from Warsaw, *Matysiakowie*, first broadcast in 1956, is Poland's longest-running radio drama series. It airs every Saturday for 25 minutes on Polskie Radio 1 and, despite a recent fall in listening figures, remains a national treasure.

W Jezioranach. Another soap, this one set in the fictional village of its title, *W Jezioranach* is rather like a rural version of *Matysiakowie*. First aired in 1960, the half-hour show is broadcast once a week on Polskie Radio 1

Radio ZET. Set up in 1990 in Warsaw, delivering a menu of chart hits on regular rotation.

Radio KOLOR. A station founded in 1992, catering for female listeners and lovers of black music.

RMF FM. Poland's most popular commercial radio station was also its first, established in January 1990 in Kraków. Tune in for pop music and chat.

6.1.4 New media: Poland online

Surf's up

Internet use in Poland has risen rapidly in recent years. More than half the population now subscribes to an online service provider, and the popularity of the Net has even been significant enough to reduce television set ownership. Access to the Internet is cheap here in comparison with other European nations. Subscribers have a bewildering array of Internet service providers – more than 300 – from which to choose, each offering a variety of different connection types and packages. Neostrada, Aster, Netia and UPC are amongst the big names in the marketplace.

Have broadband, will shop

Statistics from the Organisation for Economic Co-operation and Development (OECD) suggest that the Internet is fast becoming an integral part of daily life for many in Poland. An initial reluctance to shop on the Web seems to have passed, with seven out of ten Poles now buying goods online more than once a year, although the figures also reveal the majority of these shoppers to be from younger age groups. The most popular goods for purchase are video games, clothing, telephones, computers and books, although the online markets for travel and food show growth. A significant number of Poles also frequent the blogosphere, with more than three million reading or writing a blog on a daily basis. Children are particularly blog-happy.

6.2 Communications

Poland's communications network – its roads, railways and postal system – is making good progress after years in which it lagged behind Western Europe. Gradually, as the investment grows, the country becomes more navigable, its people more connected.

6.2.1 Keeping in touch: posting letters and making calls

Past the parcel: key dates in Poland's postal service

1558 King Zygmunt II August set up a permanent postal route between Kraków and Venice.

1583 King Stefan Batory introduced a flat postal rate of four *groszy* for letters sent over any distance in Poland – the world's first uniform postal rate.

Late 18th century King Stanisław August Poniatowski issued every postman (*pocztylion*) with an official uniform and post horn.

1860 The first Polish postage stamp was issued for use in the Congress Kingdom of Poland; five years later, Polish stamps were withdrawn and replaced by Russian ones.

1991 The young Polish parliament passes the Telecommunications Law creating Poczta Polska.

Postal service pushes the envelope

Poland's current national postal service, Poczta Polska, was created in 1991 when the new Telecommunications Law split the old, state-controlled PTT (the Post, Telegraph and Telephone Ministry) into its various parts. The organisation is vast, employing more than 100,000 people, and maintaining over 8,000 post offices, 4,500 vehicles and 50,000 post boxes. However, the entire postal system is experiencing a period of transition, opening itself up to competition as per EU directives. As a consequence, a growing number of private, foreign-owned courier companies, such as DHL, FedEx and UPS, have increased their operations in the parcel delivery market. Similarly, Poczta Polska's monopoly on letters weighing less than 50 grammes is changing with the advent of deregulation.

I hope you're not in a hurry

The country's postal service doesn't enjoy the best reputation. Letters and parcels are frequently delayed; some disappear altogether. Complaints about the

excessive bureaucracy in the post office, where official transactions can be protracted and complex, are common. Long, slow-moving queues represent a familiar post office experience for many Poles, although some branches do now operate a ticket system that enables the user to do other things (go for a coffee, read a paper, take a short holiday) whilst they wait.

Triumph of telephony: the phone network

When Poland's major national telecommunications provider, Telekomunikacja Polska (TP), was born in 1991 its first task was to sort out the underfunded, poorly developed mess left behind by the PTT, the Communist government's post and telephone ministry. Some parts of the country had no phone connection at all. Given such inauspicious roots, TP has performed remarkably well – today, the telephone network, after much restructuring and foreign investment (of both money and expertise) is of the highest standard. TP remains the dominant force, although faces healthy competition from other fixed-line operators such as Netia, Aster and Dialog.

An easy cell: mobile phones

The Poles have embraced mobile phones – for talking and texting – with great alacrity. Indeed, the overwhelming majority of the population owns at least one *komórka*. The country's main mobile operators are T-Mobile, Play, Plus and Orange, all of which offer predominantly contract-based deals. Prepaid (pay-as-you-go) mobiles from the likes of TAK TAK, Heyah and Simplus are also widely available.

In the phone booth

Telephone booths are slowly disappearing in Poland in the age of the mobile phone, although they can still be found on most streets. They come in two versions: one managed by TP, for which you have to buy a phone card, available from most news stands and petrol stations; and another operated by Netia, which only accept coins – 50 *groszy* for a two-minute daytime local call and one *złoty* per minute for daytime calls between cities.

Emergency numbers

997 Police
998 Fire Department
999 Ambulance
112 All emergencies

6.2.2 Poland on the move: transport

The speed limits

Built-up areas
50 km/hr

Outside built-up areas
90 km/hr

Dual carriageways
100 km/hr

Dual express carriageways
110 km/hr

Motorways
140 km/hr

The road network's bumpy ride

Poland has a comprehensive network of roads (covering almost 400,000 km in all), including a web of expressways and dual carriageways connecting all major towns and cities. Sadly, however, much of this network is in a dilapidated state. A lack of public funding in the wake of communism's retreat saw the already neglected infrastructure deteriorating further. Bureaucracy didn't help; new projects had to negotiate tangles of red tape before any ground could be broken. Finally, following the country's entry into the EU, with its attendant funding, money is being spent, although much remains to be done. In particular, Poland is developing its rather scant motorway network.

Out in rural areas, bedevilled by potholes and frequented by archaic agricultural vehicles, the roads will no doubt present a dangerous and frustrating driving experience for years to come. The problems on the road surface are compounded by poor street lighting. Where lighting exists it is often weak, even in the big cities, and drivers are legally obliged to drive with dipped headlights.

Driving habits and laws

The Poles aren't known for their genteel driving skills. Indicating, road signs, traffic lights and speed limits are all regularly treated as something of an inconvenience. This, coupled with the poorly maintained roads, accounts for the dozen or so deaths that occur on the country's roads every day. Strict traffic regulations attempt to deal with the problem: making a mobile phone call whilst at the wheel is banned (unless it's 'hands free'); the use of seat belts is compulsory, front and back; and there is zero tolerance for drink-driving, with a blood alcohol level over 0.5 mg/l being punishable by up to two years in prison.

Slowly does it: the rail network

With over 26,500 kilometres of track, Poland's rail network covers almost the entire country. The state-owned national rail company behind it, Polskie Koleje Państwowe (PKP), was founded in 1918. On the whole, train travel is efficient and, by Western European standards, inexpensive. However, trains are often overcrowded and unremittingly slow, even on intercity lines. There are no high-speed lines; most of the track is too old, having been laid during the country's Communist era or, in some cases, before the Second World War. Plans are afoot to build a new high-speed line linking Warsaw with Łódź, Wrocław and Poznań, and there are also proposals to renovate the CMK (Centralna Magistrala Kolejowa) line that connects Warsaw with Kraków and Katowice, thereby shortening journey times.

They seek him here...

'Mr. Prawo Jazdy' was a famously notorious and elusive Polish driver, for a while at least. Police in the Irish Republic spent months searching for him in connection with a host of unpaid parking and speeding fines. He was registered on the police database as having over 50 different aliases and addresses. The mystery was finally solved when someone quietly pointed out that *Prawo Jazdy* was, in fact, Polish for 'driving licence', the phrase that appears at the top of all such forms of ID.

The national carrier

Polskie Linie Lotnicze, more commonly known as LOT Polish Airlines, is one of the world's oldest extant airlines, having first taken to the skies in 1929. The company, and its fleet of 55 aircraft, is in the process of being privatised.

Beneath Warsaw's Streets

The Warsaw Metro (Metro warszawskie) is Poland's only underground rapid transit system, consisting of a single north/south line about 23 km in length and connecting 21 stations in all. Proposals to build the underground network were first mooted in 1918, but the years of war and insufficient funding meant that the inhabitants of the capital had to wait until 1995 before they got to use its fast and efficient service. A second - east/west - line is under construction beneath the city. Long-held plans for an underground system in Kraków remain, as yet, unfulfilled.

Train, bus and tram: regional transport

In line with EU demands, many of Poland's regional train networks have passed from the PKP to Przewozy Regionalne, a limited company owned by the 16 regional authorities. Local towns and cities also have highly functional bus and tram services, usually owned by the local authority, although some routes in certain towns are now in the hands of private operators. Most town and city transport runs between 5.30am and 11pm, whilst the larger cities provide night bus services.

Air travel

Warsaw is the hub for air travel in Poland. The city's Frederic Chopin International Airport (Lotnisko Chopina w Warszawie) handles over eight million passengers each year and accommodates three out of every four international flights landing in Poland. The airport is also home to the national carrier, LOT, which operates flights to most international destinations and domestic services from Warsaw to other major cities in the country.

184

1. Identity: the foundations of Polish culture   2. Literature and philosophy   3. Art, architecture and design   4. Music, theatre, and comedy   5. Cinema and fashion   **6. Media and communications**   7. Food and drink   8. Living culture: the state of modern Poland

Baltic bound: Poland's ports

The main Polish ports are Gdańsk, Gdynia, and Świnoujście, which operate regular passenger ferry connections from Poland to Denmark and Sweden, and are also the country's most important centres for importing and exporting cargo, a good deal of which is handled by the Polish Merchant Navy (Polska Marynarka Handlowa) and its 57 ships. The Port of Gdańsk alone, which now competes with neighbouring ports in Germany and the Netherlands having recently completed its Deepwater Container Terminal, deals with more than 27 million tonnes of goods each year.

The key airports

Warsaw Frederic Chopin International (Lotnisko Chopina w Warszawie).

Kraków Jana Pawła II International (Kraków Airport im. Jana Pawła II).

Katowice International (Międzynarodowy Port Lotniczy Katowice-Pyrzowice).

Gdańsk Lech Wałęsa International (Port Lotniczy Gdańsk im. Lecha Wałęsy).

Copernicus, Wrocław (Port Lotniczy Wrocław im. Mikołaja Kopernika).

Poznań-Ławica Henryk Wieniawski (Port Lotniczy Poznań-Ławica im. Henryka Wieniawskiego).

7 Food and Drink

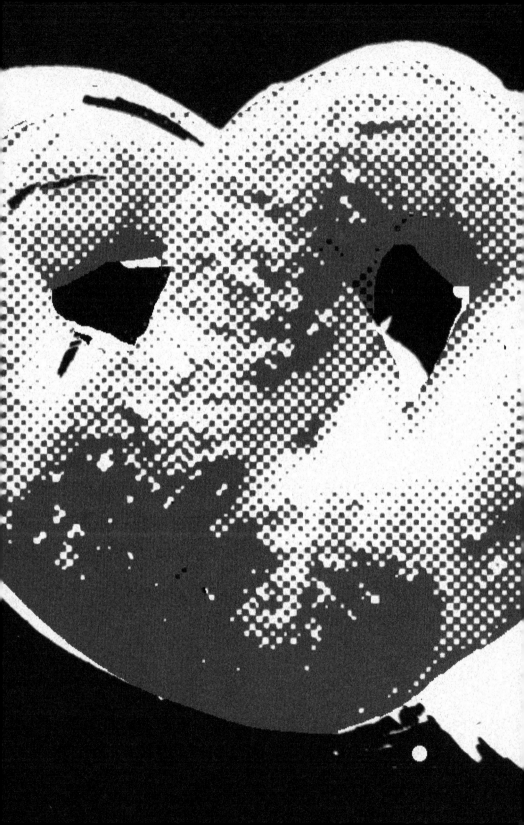

7.1 Food

Leave your preconceptions behind – Poland has one of the tastiest cuisines in Europe. Admittedly, the carb-fuelled cliché of solid cabbage and potato-heavy food has its place, but it's only one element in a complex menu of home cooking that features Hungarian, Jewish, German, Lithuanian and Russian influences and the refined legacy of Renaissance courts.

7.1.1 *Kuchnia Polska*: the changing culture of Polish food

The melting pot

Poland's place at the heart of Europe has been fundamental to its cuisine. The ebb and flow of foreign overlords brought the adoption of exotic traditions, flavours and techniques. From the Austro-Hungarian Empire, with its cakes and pastries, the Poles inherited their sweet tooth, whilst the Jewish kitchens of Warsaw gave them a taste for bagels. From Hungary they took goulash, and from the Ukraine its borscht.

Similarly, the Polish countryside has always played its part as a vast natural larder. The inland lakes, fresh-running rivers and Baltic coastline have been fished for millennia, whilst the fertile central plains produced the wheat, barley and rye that was (and still is) transformed into bread and pasta. Wild boar, deer, bison and feathered game were once plentiful in the dense forests of the north and south, supplemented by bountiful harvests of mushrooms (considered a good meat substitute), wild fruit, nuts and honey. And, of course, there's the tradition of drying or preserving foods in salt or vinegar – sauerkraut being the most famous – ensuring year-round sustenance.

Having tenaciously survived post-war attempts to annihilate its national cuisine (the Communist regime rationed food, suppressed regional menus, closed restaurants and caused food shortages with corruption and collectivisation), today Poland is enjoying a culinary renaissance. Celebrity chefs are playing their part (the Poles are as enamoured with TV cookery shows as the rest of the Western world), a slow food movement is gaining momentum and the country's palate grows increasingly sophisticated (in urban areas particularly), juxtaposing traditional dishes with innovative and modern Polish (MoPo) or fusion cuisine. Bon appetit or *smacznego!*

Italian vegetable roots

Big dress: tick. Dowry: tick. Celery: tick. When Bona Sforza arrived in Kraków in 1918 ahead of marrying King Zygmunt I she (or her chefs at least) brought a whole new range of vegetables to Poland. Such was the Italian influence on the Polish diet that several of the names still used by Poles for vegetables derive from an Italian root: *pomidor*, tomato, comes from *pomodoro*; *cebula*, onion, from *cipolla*; and the collective term for leeks, carrots and celery is *włoszczyzna*, from *Wlochy*, the Polish word for Italy. And it wasn't just veg: Sforza is also credited with helping to introduce *babka*, a close relation of *panettone*. *Babka* is actually the Polish word for 'grandmother' – baked in a bundt tin, the bread is said to resemble the shape of an old woman's skirt.

A few key dates in Polish cuisine

Tenth century: The chronicles of Abraham ben Jacob describe a territory abundant in 'grains and meats and honeys and fish'.

Middle Ages: Historic trading links with the Middle East introduced juniper, pepper, nutmeg and other spices that became kitchen staples, used for flavour but also to mask the scent of old meat.

1518: When Italian-born Queen Bona Sforza married King Zygmunt I, she took an entourage of Italian chefs to Poland. They introduced a variety of vegetables including lettuces, leeks and cabbage, as well as more delicate recipes for soups and stews.

1573: When Poland fell under the brief rule of Frenchman Henri de Valois, an appreciation of rich and buttery sauces grew, influenced by French chefs at the royal court.

1682: Publication of the first Polish cookbook, *Compendium Ferculorum albo zebranie potraw*.

1989: When the Communist government fell, long-suppressed Polish cuisine initiated a resurgence aided by old recipes and renewed access to fresh local ingredients.

The national dishes

Bigos. A hunter's stew comprising layers of cabbage or sauerkraut, mixed meats, game and sausage, which is slow cooked and reheated several times to intensify the flavour (it's not for the faint-hearted). Adam Mickiewicz (see section 2.1.4) eulogised the dish in *Pan Tadeusz:* 'In the pots warmed the *bigos*; mere words cannot tell. Of its wondrous taste, colour and marvellous smell'.

Gołąbki: The 'little pigeons' are actually cabbage leaves stuffed with meat and rice and then baked. According to legend, King Kazimierz IV fed *gołąbki* to his army before the battle of Malbork in 1465. They won, apparently thanks to the high nutritional content of the dish.

Pierogi: Numerous food festivals celebrate the ravioli-like dumplings stuffed with both savoury and sweet fillings.

Marek Widomski. Founder of the Culinary Institute in Kraków who has done much to promote native culinary traditions in the post-Communist era.

Joseph Seeletso. Poland's first black celebrity chef has a ten-minute slot on *Good Morning TVN*, an avid following and a résumé featuring Michael Jackson, Edyta Górniak and Bill Gates.

Magda Gessler. The presenter of *Kuchenne rewolucje* owns several restaurants, where she is known for fusion dishes such as deep-fried carp ribbons with wasabi and horseradish.

Karol Okrasa. A TV chef who also runs the kitchen at Platter in the Intercontinental Hotel, Warsaw, Okrasa gives a contemporary spin to traditional seasonal ingredients such as game, wild mushrooms and millet.

Żurek: A sour rye soup often served as a winter warmer with sausages and potatoes.

Barszcz: Polish *borscht*, a ruby-red beetroot soup of uncertain origin – the Russians, Ukrainians and Polish all stake a claim.

Makowiec: One of the most popular Polish cakes, for which poppy seeds are layered between sweet dough laden with almonds, orange peel and raisins. Particularly popular at Christmas.

What's in the larder?

The stove remains at the heart of the Polish home, pressed into service to sate the country's long-held taste for slow cooking and baking. There's an

Magda Gessler

emphasis on fresh ingredients; a particular love of fish, pork, game, seasonal fruit, wild mushrooms, cereals, beetroot, spices, sour cream, dill and horseradish – the staples of Polish food. Pork has long been the most popular meat, but the old recipes with game (including partridge, quail and venison), often marinated in a traditional mix of juniper, bay leaves, allspice and cloves, remain popular. Fish comes a close second to pork in popularity, not least because the Catholic Church traditionally forbade meat on fasting days.

Soup remains a vital component of almost every meal, with a recipe for every occasion and season. Chilled fruit and vegetable soups are consumed in summer; whilst the winter brings variants thickened by potatoes or grains. Sweets are similarly popular, from *sernik* (cheesecake) to *tort czekoladowy*, a rich chocolate and almond torte.

Bread (*chleb*) still carries huge dietary and cultural significance in Poland. Important guests and newlyweds are still greeted with bread and salt, and its deep-rooted religious connection remains; the reverence paid in old poems and folksongs is still pertinent. Sourdough, of thick

crust and soft centre, is the most popular variety. Look out too for *obwarzanek* (a relative of the bagel), *chleb górski* (mountain bread) and *prądnicki* (rye bread).

A love affair with the sausage

A staple of the Polish diet, *kiełbasa* is a generic term applied to all manner of sausages, including smoked, uncooked, mild and spicy. Typically they're made from pork, although turkey, lamb and venison versions are also found. The earliest record of *kiełbasa* dates to the 18th century, describing a thick, darkly coloured and heavily smoked sausage of considerable length. There are various different characters within the *kiełbasa* family:

Kabanos. A thin air-dried sausage seasoned with black pepper and sometimes caraway seeds. The name is derived from *kaban*, an archaic (and now defunct) word in a regional dialect, which means boar (male pig), but it can also be made with turkey and chicken, depending on region. *Kabanos* is almost always eaten cold as an appetizer.

Krakowska. A popular and chunky pork affair, named after Kraków and often found in salads and sandwiches, the *Krakowska* is made to a 16th century recipe. It's usually seasoned with allspice, coriander and garlic and then packed into a large casing before being smoked.

Wiejska. A smoked sausage made of pork and veal with marjoram and garlic. The name means 'country', from the Polish *wieś*.

Biała. A white sausage made from pork and beef that is cooked or fried before being eaten. Commonly served at Easter with *żurek*.

Lisiecka: Made in Liszki in the Małopolska region, the Protected Geographical Indication (PGI) rated *Lisiecka* is lightly seasoned with garlic and pepper before being smoked over the wood of alder, beech or fruit trees to create a distinctive smell and flavour.

Four excellent cheeses

Oscypek. Poland's most famous cheese is made from salted ewe's milk and then smoked. Originally produced by Wallachian shepherds circa 1416, today *Oscypek* has Protected Designation of Origin (PDO) status. Often eaten with red wine or smoked fish.

Bundz. Another one made from sheep's milk, *Bundz* has a mild flavour and a texture similar to cottage cheese.

Bryndza. A soft, spreadable PDO ewe's milk cheese made in the southerly Podhale region since 1527. For a while *Bryndza* was used as legal tender.

Koryciński. A hard cheese made from cow's milk and named after the town of Korycin in north-eastern Poland.

194

Give us this day: bread facts

Each Pole consumes an average of 100kg of bread each year.

The Museum of Bread opened at Radzionków, Silesia, in 1992.

Some bakers still mark their bread with the sign of the cross.

Bread that falls onto the floor must be picked up and kissed.

Convention dictates that throwing away old bread could bring bad luck or hunger.

Polish housewives were traditionally advised not to quarrel when bread was rising, should the bread take offence and fail to rise or fall.

A loaf of *Prądnicki,* a chewy PGI rye bread originally made for the local clergy by bakers in the *Prądnicki* district of Kraków in the 15th century, weighs in at 5kg.

Despite the best efforts of the post-war government to homogenise regional food around Poland, each province retains its own menu. And, as the movement to celebrate this regional diversity grows, so the old recipes and foodstuffs – a butch but surprisingly well-flavoured group – find themselves embraced with renewed enthusiasm and served up as an integral facet of Polish cultural identity.

Pomerania

The Baltic coastline and crystal clear lakes stock Pomerania's menu with a preponderance of fish. Herring (*śledź*) is taken from Gdańsk, the prime fishing port, and served in various ways: pickled, with soured cream, with apples and cream, and with onion. Dill, a favourite herb, thrives in the damp climate and is used in the likes of *łupacz gotowany*, a sauce topping for haddock. From the Kashubian rivers come trout (*pstrąg*), simply grilled, and summer salmon (*łosoś*), smoked and served with fresh asparagus. In Toruń, on Pomerania's southern border, *pierniki*, a soft gingerbread, can be traced back to the 13th century.

Wielkopolska

Greater Poland shares a very important ingredient with its southern neighbour Silesia - the potato (*pyry*). They're made into dumplings, noodles, fritters, flour, bread and even desserts. *Placki ziemniaczane* (potato pancakes), a staple in the Second World War when food was scarce, are a long held favourite, devoured today with sour cream – and paprika – or apple sauce. In *pyzy* the potatoes are mashed and grated, formed into dumplings and served up with a thick aromatic stew. Dumplings are also made from plums (*knedle ze śliwkami*), encased in potato dough and stuffed with sugar and cinnamon. In Poznań they make *Rogal świętomarciński*, a sweet, crescent-shaped pastry filled with a mixture of white poppy seeds, raisins, nuts and candied fruit.

195

Warmia-Masuria and Podlaskie

The cool waters of north-eastern Poland's myriad lakes harbour sizeable pike, traditionally fried or grilled and served with chopped hard-boiled eggs and a garnish of parsley or a rich sauce made with red wine and raisins. The region's vast Suwalszczyzna forest is carpeted with mushrooms (Poland is the largest producer of wild mushrooms in Europe), which are collected and used in *zupa ze świeżych grzybów* (wild mushroom soup with pasta), *duszone grzyby* (sautéed wild mushrooms) and *zrazy* (steak rolled and stuffed with mushrooms). With Lithuania and Russia close by, foreign influences have also helped shape the local diet, particularly the *pierogi*, a ravioli-style dish that began life as peasant food but soon climbed the social ladder. *Pierogi* fillings include *z serem* (cheese), *ruskie* (Russian – a combination of curd cheese, mashed potato and fried onion), *z kapustą* (sauerkraut) and *z mięsem* (minced meat). Sweet versions feature fruit or curd cheese mixed with candied fruit. The savoury version is topped with breadcrumbs fried in butter or sour cream; the sweet with sugar.

Masovia

Masovia's prime agricultural lands stake a claim as the birthplace of *bigos* (see section 7.1.1), served here with rye bread to soak up the flavours and vodka to aid digestion. A proliferation of forests has given the region a cuisine based on fruit (30 per cent of Poland's orchards are in Masovia) and meat. *Gęś z owocami* is a popular Masovian dish – goose stuffed with aromatic fruit (often prunes, apricots and oranges) and served with spiced red cabbage. Another local recipe features fillets of pork marinated in wine, marjoram and caraway seeds and then stuffed with prunes before baking. Typically, such a

Dark secrets

Renowned for its richly
fertile black soils,
the village of Czarna
Wieś (Black Village)
once supplied the
royal kitchens with
vegetables. Today,
the dark earth (and
the village) have been
subsumed by Kraków's
cityscape.

dish is served with *ćwikła*, a beetroot salad, or *gryczana*, buckwheat kasha.

Małopolska

Beyond the urbane restaurants, cafés and food festivals of Kraków, the southern forests of Małopolska teem with game, including the famous Kraków duck. Pigs, cattle and sheep graze in the foothills of the Tatra Mountains; the prized milk of the sheep is used to make *oscypek* and *bundz* cheese. Up in the mountains, meat – usually grilled – forms the key component of the *górale* (highlander) diet. Popular sweets from Małopolska include *sernik* (cheesecake), topped with vanilla crème, and succulent apple pie (*szarlotka*).

Silesia

Chin-burningly good soup

The name of the Silesian
soup *parzybroda*
translates roughly as
'chin scald', a name
derived from the diner's
reckless urge to wolf
it down whilst piping
hot, such are the soup's
delicious properties.

Silesia is home to the *kluski śląskie*, a diminutive dimpled potato dumpling. Typically, they're served with a meat sauce, or *rolada z modrą kapustą*, a stuffed rolled steak with red cabbage, fried bacon, onion and allspice traditionally eaten as part of Sunday lunch. The region also revels in *żurek*, the soup that has become a national institution with its garlic and marjoram aromas. Made with vegetable stock and a fermented rye mixture, the steaming broth is garnished with hard-boiled eggs and accompanied by *biała* sausage. *Parzybroda* is another traditional Silesian soup, this one made from cabbage, potato, bacon and caraway. For dessert, the Silesians are big on *makówki*: ground poppy seeds, honey, raisins and nuts mixed together, placed on thin slices of sweet bread and then topped with milk.

1. Identity: the
foundations
of Polish culture

2. Literature
and philosophy

3. Art, architecture
and design

4. Music, theatre,
and comedy

5. Cinema
and fashion

6. Media and
communications

7. Food and drink

8. Living culture:
the state of
modern Poland

7.1.3 Food rituals: eating, feasting and shopping

From no-go to Mo-Po

Restaurants offered a very limited dining experience during Poland's years under Soviet rule. Rationing limited supply and everything was monitored. There were diktats on how to prepare food, including ingredient quantities, and chefs were presented with restrictive, uninspiring menus that changed little with the seasons. When the borders reopened in the 1990s, previously unobtainable ingredients and styles of cooking became available in Poland. It all gave rise to the re-interpretation of traditional dishes, a cuisine dubbed Modern Polish, or Mo-Po.

Meals in, meals out

Social gatherings in Poland (of which there are many) invariably involve eating. Most of the dining happens in the home; there is no great tradition of eating out. Historically, few could afford meals out, with the exception of trips to the milk bar (see below). Today, whilst older generations continue to entertain at home, younger Poles dine out occasionally, when they're as likely to choose Italian, Mexican or even Japanese food as they are Polish. The reputation of restaurants in cities such as Kraków, Poznań and Wrocław grows all the time (most cities now even have vegetarian restaurants, once viewed as something of an oddity), even whilst takeaway food also increases in popularity and the likes of McDonald's become as ubiquitous here as elsewhere.

Meal times

Poland, like much of the world, breaks dining down into three square meals a day. However, the midday lunch taken by other nations remains a relatively alien concept here. Instead, Poles tend to eat breakfast, an early dinner and a late supper. A second breakfast, *drugie śniadanie*, or light late-afternoon meal, *podwieczorek* (literally 'just before evening'), is also customary.

Śniadanie. Breakfast is fast and light, typically comprising bread (wheat or rye), topped with cheese, ham or sausage and taken with a cup of tea.

Obiad. The main meal of the day is typically eaten between four and five in the afternoon. Usually there will be soup, a meat dish, potatoes and a portion of vegetables or salad, followed by dessert.

Kolacja. Supper is rather like an ambitious version of breakfast. Portions are larger and feature a greater selection of dishes, such as cold meats and *kiełbasa*, beetroot, cucumber or *kasha* (buckwheat) salads, egg dishes, bread and cheeses. *Kolacja* is often a leisurely affair, used to catch up on the day's events.

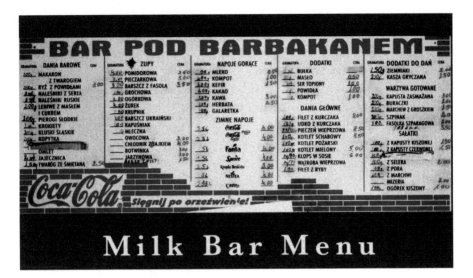

Milk Bar Menu

Dining out with the proletariat

The *Bar Mleczny* (milk bar) is an irrepressible relic of Poland's Communist past. Subsidised by the government, they enabled low-paid workers to have a meal out (the bars are actually more like cafés, selling dairy-led food as well as milk). Today, the food at Poland's state-subsidised milk bars remains basic, quick, cheap and filling. They're worth a visit for quirky ambience alone.

Tips for tipping

On average, Poles tip ten per cent of the total bill. If you say *dziękuję* (thank you) after paying for the meal, it will be assumed that you do not expect/want your change back.

Dining etiquette

Gość w dom, Bóg w dom is an old Polish proverb that translates as 'Guest in the home, God in the home'. Make no mistake – if you're invited into a Polish home, a huge effort will be made to make you feel welcome. Indeed, Poles are renowned for being generous and gregarious hosts. If you are lucky enough to be asked over for dinner, remember the following:

- Punctuality is vital.
- It is considered good manners to offer help with preparing the meal and with clearing up afterwards.
- Wait for your host to invite you to start eating.
- Expect frequent toasting. The first toast (made with hard liquor, usually vodka) is offered by the host; it is customary to then reciprocate with your own toast later in the meal.
- Try a little of everything offered and indulge in a second helping – it's only polite.
- A small gift of flowers, pastries or sweets for the host is appreciated but not obligatory. Don't be extravagant or you might embarrass the host. If you do take flowers give an odd number of stems (they will be counted); an even number is reserved for funerals.

199

Feast foods

With eating and preparing food at the heart of almost all social occasions, the Poles need little excuse for a feast. As they're fond of saying, *jedzcie, pijcie i popuszczajcie pasa* (eat, drink and loosen your belt). There are certain feasts that enjoy almost universal participation throughout the country:

Tłusty czwartek (Fat Thursday). On the last Thursday before the start of lent, Poland goes mad for the *pączki*, a doughnut filled with rose petal jam. Around 100 million are devoured each year – that's about two and a half per person. *Pączki* are believed to bring good luck for the remainder of the year, and are duly often given as gifts.

Wielkanoc. Easter is celebrated with a lavish breakfast. Small baskets of food are taken to church to be blessed on Holy Saturday and then eaten a day later. The typical Easter breakfast features cold meats, *kiełbasa*, herring, salmon, vegetables, salads, egg dishes and cakes, especially *mazurek* (an iced pastry) and *babka*. Many of the foods carry a symbolism: eggs represent life; the lamb is Christ; bread is symbolic of Jesus; and horseradish sauce recalls his sacrifice.

Święty Marcin. The Feast of St Martin on 11th November has a particular importance in the Wielkopolska region, where they eat *rogale* (see Wielkopolska, above) by the ton.

Wigilia. The Christmas Eve supper is the most important feast in the calendar. After a day of fasting, the meal begins when the first star appears in the sky. An exchange of good wishes is followed by the breaking and sharing of *opłatek*, an unleavened Christmas wafer. Tradition requires the feast's 12 dishes (one for each apostle) to be meat-free (fish is allowed), a custom still generally observed today. Carp, fried or set in aspic, always takes centre stage.

Boże Narodzenie. There are no die-hard traditions on Christmas Day, but roasted duck (with apples) is popular, as are goose and chicken. It's a time for indulgence, with richer dishes than on Wigilia and plenty of sweets.

Sylwester. Poles party hard on New Year's Eve, the feast day of St Sylwester. For sustenance, typical dishes include bigos, served, naturally, with vodka. Bread is baked in the shape of rabbits, geese and cows to ensure good luck for the year ahead.

Shopping for food

Queuing for basic supplies is a thing of the past. Western-style supermarkets are widespread although many Poles still prefer to buy fresh produce from speciality shops and local markets, which are usually held on Thursdays, Fridays and/or Saturdays. Corner shops are found everywhere, stock virtually everything and still operate as a meeting place for the local community.

Bath fresh

To ensure freshness, the Wigilia carp was traditionally kept alive, often swimming in the bathtub until the moment of cooking arrived.

Are we expecting someone else?

Many Poles still set an empty place for dinner at Wigilia, ensuring that any unexpected guest may have a place at the table and will be treated as a member of the family.

7.2 Drink

Sorry to disappoint but the Poles drink more tea than anything else. Alcohol consumption has been a problem in the past, particularly amongst the over-40 age group, but the perception of the Poles as heavy drinkers is misplaced.

7.2.1 Drinking habits

Blind disobedience

Buying a bottle of good vodka could be difficult in the Communist era, with rationing and food coupons in place, and so the Poles set up their own stills. The perpetrators were demonised as enemies of the state. Posters carried the slogan 'Homemade vodka is the cause of blindness', and homes were raided and the producers locked up.

Sobering statistics

Alcohol consumption is falling year by year in Poland and the patterns of drinking are changing. Vodka, for so long the national drink, is falling back behind beer and other drinks in popularity. Indeed, even whilst it would still be a mistake to make a toast with anything but vodka, today younger Poles are far more likely to drink beer, wine or cocktails on an evening out.

Wine sales in Poland have been increasing steadily over the last decade, a trend often attributed to rising wealth and wine's attendant social kudos as much as to increased choice. The consumption of beer (Poland's 'favourite' alcoholic drink according to the relevant surveys) is similarly buoyant, the sales helped by the emergence of British-style pubs which, along with more traditional cafés and bars, give drinkers in towns and cities a large choice of venues in which to imbibe. Nevertheless, most Poles are more likely to drink at home.

None of this, of course, lessens the depth of vodka's cultural roots. Consumption may be falling, led by the trend for a healthier lifestyle and a growing awareness of alcohol-related problems, but vodka remains the default drink for any celebratory occasion. Every Polish home has a bottle stashed somewhere, pressed into service with the arrival of visitors. A toast also seals business deals and celebrates family gatherings and holidays.

The legal situation

The legal age for buying alcohol in Poland is 18 years, for which valid ID is required. Be warned; the police take a hard line on public inebriation. Anyone arrested for being drunk in a public place may find themselves committed to a drying out clinic. In the larger cities, where the recent influx of foreign stag parties has brought with it the usual drunken antics, the authorities work to balance the Polish taste for relative sobriety (even if only in appearance) with the need to grow the tourist economy.

7.2.2 What do the Poles drink?

"THE THREE MOST ASTONISHING THINGS IN THE PAST HALF-CENTURY HAVE BEEN THE BLUES, CUBISM AND POLISH VODKA."
Pablo Picasso

Wonderful wódka

Toast by saying *na zdrowie* (health) and then slug it down in one – *do dna* (to the bottom).

Woda translates as 'water' and the diminutive *ka* means 'little'; put them together for *wódka*.

When King Jan Olbracht issued a decree permitting every citizen to make vodka in 1546, distilling commenced on a vast scale.

In 1534 scientist Stefan Falimierz said that vodka could increase fertility and awaken lust.

A *kulawka* is a toasting goblet that can only be set down once its contents have been consumed, as the vessel has to rest on its rim.

Vodka

Polish vodka enjoys a worldwide reputation for quality. Traditionally made from grain (more so than potatoes in Poland), it's a drink to be taken neat, chilled and in one gulp. Despite Russian protestations, it seems the Poles may lay legitimate claim to the drink's origins, not least because the oldest surviving document featuring the word *wódka*, dating to 1405, is Polish. Fruit, herbs and spices were used to make the drink palatable when commercial distillation began in the 16th century, a practice that continued into the modern era. Poland's distilleries were requisitioned by the state in the post-war era and vodka was rationed. Today, the industry is in private hands once more, and the drink has been successfully remarketed as a luxury product (although rougher variants remain). The taste for flavoured versions persists – indeed, there are more than 300 flavoured Polish vodkas on the market.

The vodka that makes you thinner

The Hierochloe odorata, as used in Żubrówka vodka, contains coumarin, a naturally occurring chemical sometimes used as a blood thinner. The compound has been banned in the USA and certain other countries, but, thankfully, coumarin-free versions of Żubrówka are available for export.

Three flavoured Polish vodkas

Myśliwska. Hunter's vodka flavoured with juniper berries – not unlike gin to taste.

Wiśniówka. Rectified vodka flavoured with cherries.

Pieprzówka. Vodka imbued with paprika and black pepper.

Five famous Polish vodkas

Żubrówka. Perhaps the most beloved of Poland's mass-produced vodkas, Żubrówka is made with rye and infused with hierochloe grass (also called bison grass after its prime patron) from the Białowieźa forest. A blade of bison grass appears in each bottle. Enjoy it straight up or with two-parts apple juice to make a *szarlotka* (apple pie).

Wyborowa. In 1823 Hartwig Kantorowicz entered his brew into a competition to find the best vodka in Poland – and won. The panel proclaimed it *wyborowa* (exquisite) and the label stuck. Produced from rye grain grown in the village of Turew, Wielkopolska, Wyborowa continues to be made in small batches and is quadruple-distilled to create a well-rounded, smooth and fresh drink.

Chopin. Considered a luxury brand, Chopin is a potato-based vodka, distilled four times to remove all impurities, and is praised for its complex taste and texture.

Belvedere. With a subtle sweetness and a smooth clean finish, Belvedere is a single-grain, quadruple-distilled vodka made in the small town of Żyrardów in the Mazovian plains west of Warsaw. It's named for the palace that used to house Polish royalty.

Starka. Aged for several years in oak barrels, Starka develops a warm yellowy colour.

Beer

The Poles have been brewing (and drinking) beer since the Middle Ages. Today they favour a strong (around 5.5 per cent alcohol) lager-style beer, although recent years have witnessed a revival in older forms – honey beers or wheat beers, as well as stouts, porters and other dark brews. This revival has accompanied the return of Poland's brewing industry to private ownership after the state control of the Communist era. The country now has several moderately sized brewers although the lion's share of consumption is drawn from three multinational-

Żywiec Porter. A so-called Baltic Porter (9.5 per cent ABV) with a sweet treacle and brown sugar aroma and flavours of toasted malt, coffee and plum. Perfect for sipping after dinner.

Rycerskie: A strong blonde lager (7 per cent ABV) from the Namysłów brewery in south-western Poland. Light and fruity with sweet malt flavours.

Tatra Pils: A Czech style Pilsner (6 per cent ABV) from the Żywiec brewery. Smooth and malty – perfect with a *pierogi*.

Perła Chmielowa: A pale lager (6.2 per cent ABV) first brewed in Lublin more than a century ago. Clean and malty aromas with floral and citrus tastes.

Tyskie Gronie. Poland's best-selling beer, a golden lager (5.6 per cent ABV), is owned by SAB Miller, although the original Tyskie brewery was founded in 1629.

owned companies – Kompania Piwowarska (SAB Miller), Żywiec (Heineken) and Okocim (Carlsberg) – producing a large number of branded beers.

Despite the dominance of the big three, microbreweries – often attached to a pub (brewpubs) – are increasingly popular in Poland, most notably in the country's south-western reaches where the historic influence of the German, Austrian and Czech taste for beer is at its strongest. Perhaps one of them will even start brewing Grodziskie in the near future. Grodziskie is (or was) an indigenous top-fermented brew made with smoked malt that slipped from production in the mid 1990s but is still viewed fondly by many, no doubt through beer-tinted spectacles.

Two beery cocktails

The Poles sometimes drink their beer mixed with other ingredients. Two hybrids in particular are popular.

Piwo z sokiem mixes beer with syrup. Blackcurrant and ginger are popular flavourings. The mix is often drunk through a straw.

Piwo grzane is warm beer flavoured with cloves, cinnamon and honey, popularly drunk during winter.

Wine

Polish wine production is spluttering back into life having all but died out in the 1990s. Small producers in Lower Silesia (one of the few regions in Poland with a realistic chance of cultivating good vines), particularly around the city of Zielona Góra where *wino* has a centuries-old history, are producing good wine encouraged by the city and regional authorities. A local wine festival in September celebrates the revival.

However, the overwhelming majority of wine drunk in Poland is still produced outside its borders. Much of it comes from Bulgaria and Hungary, with red wine more popular than white. French wine, naturally, is still the most prized. As already noted, consumption is rising, particularly

Grape expectations

Programmes have been initiated to help local farmers grasp the complexities of viniculture. The Vineyards of Małopolska scheme, in the south of Poland, has brought together 50 farmers from around Kraków and Nowy Sącz. They're experimenting with different grape varieties, choosing the vines that can cope with Poland's periodically harsh climate. As yet, they haven't produced wine for the Polish table, but it shouldn't be long before they do.

Winter wine

In winter, Poles drink *grzaniec*, a mulled wine teeming with the wonderful aromas of cloves, nutmeg and cinnamon.

amongst young adults and particularly in Poland's cities, where they drink more than twice the national average. Beer and vodka still hold sway in rural areas.

Four more from the bar

Mead. Viewed as a rather arcane tipple in most Western countries, mead (*miód pitny*) retains an important, if reduced, place in Polish drinking culture. The country has been fermenting honey and herb-infused water (wort) for a thousand years. In 966 a Spanish diplomat recently returned from Poland wrote: "The country of Mieszko I abounds in food, meat, fields and Slavonic wine and the intoxicating drinks are called meads". Today, a number of producers still make commercial mead, even whilst it isn't drunk as widely as it once was.

Goldwasser. A potent (40 per cent proof) aniseed-based liqueur flavoured with more than 20 herbs and roots (including lavender, thyme and cinnamon) and – sit down – flecks of real gold leaf. Production began in 16th century Gdańsk, led by Dutch immigrant Ambrose Vermollen. He added gold for its supposedly magical medicinal properties.

Nalewka. Aged, throat-burning (another one that's 40 per cent proof) fruit liqueurs that come in a variety of flavours, such as cherry, apricot and blackberry. Other versions include cardamom and ginger, whilst the exotic-sounding *krambambula* is a mix of honey, cinnamon and pepper. Polish custom dictates that medium and semi-dry fruit liqueurs should be served with meat dishes while the sweeter versions accompany desserts. Tradition also suggests that *nalewki* should be sipped rather than downed in one gulp.

208

1. Identity: the foundations of Polish culture | 2. Literature and philosophy | 3. Art, architecture and design | 4. Music, theatre, and comedy | 5. Cinema and fashion | 6. Media and communications | **7. Food and drink** | 8. Living culture: the state of modern Poland

Four Polish meads have been granted PDO status: Półtorak, Dwójniak, Trójniak and Czwórniak. The most popular is Trójniak: it matures for two years and is made of one-third honey. Półtorak, an amber coloured mead made from two-parts honey and one-part water, and aged in oak casks for up to ten years, is the most rare and expensive.

Knockout brew

South-eastern Poland produces the country's best-known moonshine, a plum brandy from Łącko that can reach 75 per cent alcohol content. Apparently in production since 1698, the ultra-potent (some say life-threatening) brandy is currently outlawed and thus difficult to acquire. You have to know someone who knows someone.

Soft facts

The Poles love carrot juice: Kubuś is the most popular brand.

Kwas is a cold, fizzy non-alcoholic beverage made from day-old rye bread.

Kompot, a drink made from stewed fruits, can be served hot or cold.

Benedyktynka. A rum and herb liqueur, the recipe for which is closely guarded by two Observant Brothers at Lubiń Monastery, Wielkopolska. First made in the 16th century by Bernardo Vincelli, an Italian monk, *Benedyktynka* remains an important element of Wielkopolska's culinary and cultural heritage. As the monks' marketing blurb says: 'It improves your mood'.

Soft options: tea and coffee

Tea. The Poles consume tea (*herbata*) in large quantities. Black tea (a relatively weak brew), taken with lemon and sugar but rarely with milk, is drunk at breakfast, lunch, dinner and pretty much any point in between. A dash of vodka or rum is sometimes added in winter – purely for warming, of course. Black tea accounts for 60 per cent of the tea market; the remainder is made up by green tea, herbal tea and fruit infusions. The statistics suggest that tea consumption in increasing by five to ten per cent each year; figures supported by the upsurge in the numbers of teashops in Poland's major cities. British brands, notably Lipton and Tetley, lead the market, although Poland's own Posti is also popular.

Coffee. When the Ottomans beat a hasty retreat from the Siege of Vienna in 1683, after being defeated by King Jan III Sobieski, they left their coffee behind. The Habsburgs took a liking to the brown stuff and its popularity duly spread to Poland. Even during the darkest days of Soviet rule coffee remained popular, and the coffee bars in which it was served provided a meeting place for students, intellectuals and anyone else looking for conversation. INKA, a caffeine-free ersatz coffee made from rye, barley and chicory, was developed in the face of shortages – and is still in production. Today, there are coffee shops everywhere in Poland where, typically, the drink is served strong and with a splash of milk. Coffee also finds its way into numerous desserts, from baked coffee custards and mousses to rich gateaux.

Whilst family and Church – the traditional pillars of Polish life – evolve slowly to meet the demands of the 21st century, the institutions of state, from the parliament to the police, have been dramatically reborn since Poland embarked on its Third Republic.

1. Identity: the foundations of Polish culture

2. Literature and philosophy

3. Art, architecture and design

4. Music, theatre, and comedy

5. Cinema and fashion

6. Media and communications

7. Food and drink

8. Living culture: the state of modern Poland

Finding the minorities

Poland's ethnic German population is concentrated in Silesia and Opole (see section 1.1.2), although a small community still remains in the north-east, in old East Prussia. Many in Silesia and Opole still speak a Germanised dialect of Polish. In the north-east, the Ukrainian communities resettled after the Second World War cling to their culture, notably at a celebratory biennial festival in Sopot. *Nasze Słowo*, a newspaper printed in Ukrainian in Warsaw, retains a devoted readership. Almost all of Poland's ethnic Belarusians live near the border with Belarus, around Białystok in particular, although the community is one of Poland's most integrated. The Roma community is perhaps the most rootless yet visible of Poland's ethnic minorities, and also perhaps the one subject to most prejudice.

On the move: the class structure

The social structure in Poland is rebalancing after years of upheaval. An ancient system that held the peasant masses in bondage to a small ruling elite had broken down by the early 20th century, and a new middle class of industrialists and entrepreneurs had emerged. However, the tumult of the Second World War and the subsequent years of Communist rule swept the middle classes (and any remaining aristocracy) aside.

In the Soviet era, what became the ruling elite was drawn from all sectors of society – linked by their membership of the Polish United Workers' Party. The years of communism also allied the intelligentsia – traditional defenders of Polish identity – with the working classes. Today, in post-Communist Poland, the middle class has re-emerged; led initially, if the accusations are correct, by the old Communist elite that had the advantage of good contacts and capital. The intellectual class has alienated many of its former working-class allies by accepting social and economic hardships as the 'inevitable price to pay for freedom'. Even while there is social mobility in modern Poland, the low-skilled working classes – particularly in rural areas – have been the main losers in the transition to democracy.

How multicultural is Poland?

Poland is less ethnically diverse today than at almost any other time in its history. For centuries, the region celebrated a religious and cultural mix unrivalled anywhere else in Europe, its population inclusive of large Belarusian, German, Ukrainian and Jewish communities. The Second World War annihilated the Jewish population, and post-war geopolitics moved Germans, Ukrainians and other minorities out (see section 1.2.3 for the full story). Today, almost 97 per cent of the country's population can be described as 'ethnic Polish'. Of the remainder, ethnic Germans, Ukrainians and Belarusians account for most; other minorities – Jews, Lithuanians, Tatars, Lemkos,

Karaimi, Russians and Romas – are found in smaller numbers. Notably, in recent years Poland has seen an increase in migrants from Ukraine, many of whom take up low-paid jobs.

Ties that still bind: the family unit

The family structure remains a central tenet of Polish life. Even while, as elsewhere, fewer couples now marry (some claim co-habitation brings greater financial reward from the state) and those that do are now marrying later and having fewer children than in years past, the traditional extended family unit remains prized. Many households still contain three generations of the same family, sharing the household and childcare responsibilities. Most Poles live with their parents into their mid 20s, often for financial reasons, whilst the elderly are cared for at home by family members. Consequently, nursing homes are almost non-existent. Some complain that the state, with its rather meagre pension provision, has yet to cover the shortfall for those without family to support them in later life. In a wider sense, senior citizens remain highly respected (for example, bus and train seats are still surrendered to the elderly).

Life as a Polish woman

Arguably, communism was an equaliser in the gender stakes. Nearly half the Polish workforce was female by the mid 1970s, and there were more opportunities for women in higher education (over 60 per cent of medical students in the 1980s were women), employment and male-related professions, such as architecture and engineering, than in the West. However, at the very top – in the positions of economic and political power – women were excluded. Today, women in Poland remain under-represented at decision-making levels in government (the country's first female prime minister, Hanna Suchocka, elected in 1992, stands out as a rare exception). They typically earn 35 per cent less than their male

Shrinking Poles

Polish women have an average of 1.4 children, compared to the European norm of 1.74. The rising cost of starting a family and improved career opportunities for women are blamed for the low fertility rate. The government has introduced policies aimed at increasing births and improving the quality of life for Polish families.

Mother's little helper

Maternity leave in Poland was recently increased to 20 weeks (longer for multiple births: 31 weeks for twins, 33 weeks for triplets and 35 weeks for quadruplets) and extended kindergarten opening hours and improved tax breaks for families with children were introduced. Additionally, since 2005 mothers have received a payment of 1,000 złoty for every child born.

counterparts and have
a higher unemployment
rate, even whilst they
continue to make a
major contribution
to the labour force.
Equally, Polish men
have been slower
to pitch in with the
household chores than
in other European
nations, although this is
gradually changing.

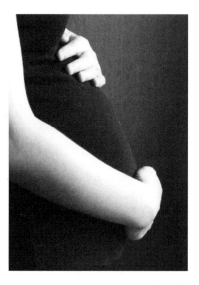

Abortion was made
illegal in most
circumstances in Poland
in the 1990s (having
been legal in the Communist era). Some estimates
suggest that over 16,000 Polish women travel abroad
to secure terminations every year; a higher number
seek underground abortions within Poland. Sterilisation
is illegal for both women and men, contraception is
relatively expensive and sex education isn't on the school
curriculum. Domestic violence against women remains
woefully under-reported, according to the relevant
surveys – many blame the gruelling courtroom experience
for victims (and this applies to rape too).

8.2 How Poland takes its religion

Mass movement

Poland is synonymous with Catholicism. For centuries the Roman Catholic Church has helped shape and define Polish identity, intensifying family relationships and providing refuge and spiritual strength. Sandwiched between Orthodox Russia and Protestant Germany, to be Catholic was to be Polish. In the years of Soviet rule, attending Mass was an act of defiance and protest, and the authorities, recognising the power of the Church, would placate religious leaders when they needed popular support (when the State didn't need Church support, religious leaders were routinely persecuted).

Even today, almost 90 per cent of the population still belongs to the Roman Catholic Church. The church pews in every Polish town and village are still full on a Sunday (although once they were overfull), and nuns, priests and other clergy are still a common sight on the streets. Sunday observance remains important, religious festivals are celebrated with vigour and a portrait of the Virgin Mary or Pope John Paul II remains standard décor in many homes. However, cracks are appearing. Post-Communist Poland is beginning to wrestle with secularisation. The role of the Church in government, particularly its insistence on conservative legislation (on abortion, sex education, etc.), has alienated many younger Poles, and the calls for a more formal separation between Church and state are growing.

Other religions in Poland

The minority religions in modern day Poland are dwarfed by the size of the Roman Catholic population. However, it wasn't always thus. Indeed, prior to the Second World War, one in ten Poles were Jewish (see section 1.2.3 for more on the fate of Poland's Jews). Today, the Jewish population is thought to be between 3,000 and 5,000. Islam is the other main non-Christian faith in modern Poland, whilst Eastern Orthodox Christians,

The Solidarity saint

The Church served as a vital forum for discussion and dissent in the years of Soviet rule – Mass being one of the few opportunities for public congress. In the 1980s, priests went as far as disseminating illegal Solidarność literature. Some paid a heavy price, notably Father Popiełuszko who was tortured and murdered for his Solidarność activity by the security police in 1984. Popiełuszko duly became a folk hero, and was beatified in 2010.

217

Jewish culture returns
The near complete destruction of Poland's Jews in the Second World War was followed by a less well-documented government campaign to drive out most of the 90,000 remaining Jews in 1968 and '69. It set the tone for an anti-Semitic undercurrent in Poland that has only really been dealt with in recent years. Today, discrimination against Judaism is declining, a change which the country's chief rabbi, Michael Schudrich, attributes in part to the teachings of tolerance by Pope John Paul II. Festivals in Kraków, Warsaw and Białystok are helping to revive Jewish music, food and culture, and Poland is also gradually becoming a place of pilgrimage for Jews (and non-Jews) in search of their roots – an estimated 70 per cent of the world's Ashkenazi Jews, for example, can trace their ancestry to Poland.

mostly living in Poland's eastern borderlands, number approximately half a million. In the Białystok region in particular, Catholics, Orthodox Christians and Muslims live side by side, whilst Silesia harbours the country's largest Protestant congregations. Pilgrimages to holy sites are very popular for all faiths: the Monastery of Jasna Góra in Częstochowa for Catholics (to see the Black Madonna, a miraculous icon); the tomb of Rabbi Elimelech in Leżajsk for Jews; and the Grabarka Sanctuary for Orthodox Christians.

Any excuse for a festival

The Poles blend ancient pagan rituals (as practised by their Western Slavic ancestors) harmoniously with religious tradition, lightening the Christian calendar's deeply serious narrative of holy days with elaborate feasts and imbibing. Saints' days (everyone marks their namesake) are celebrated with family and friends; even work colleagues will take a minute to sing *Sto Lat*, wishing a hundred years of happy life. Weddings and baptisms are famous for their intensity. They used to extend to three – and even seven – days in some communities, although busy modern lives have condensed the party down to one momentous day.

The main religious festivals

Wielkanoc (Easter). Most Poles attend mass on Ash Wednesday (Środa Popielcowa), before taking palm leaves (or handcrafted facsimiles made from pussy willow) to church for the processions on Palm Sunday (Niedziela Palmowa). On Holy Saturday (Wielka Sobota), baskets of food are taken to church and sprinkled with Holy Water. Almost every Pole then attends Resurrection Mass on Easter Sunday (Wielka Niedziela) before the blessed food is eaten. On Easter Monday (Lany Poniedzialek), the *smidges dings* ritual finds young men out on the streets dousing unsuspecting victims with water (traditionally they doused young women to increase fertility but these days it can be anyone). Two notes: the victims of *smidges dings* are not supposed to retaliate; and although a sprinkling of cologne may be considered more gentlemanly, jugs of cold water are not uncommon.

Boże Ciało (Corpus Christi). A feast held on the eighth Thursday after Easter. Processions and colourful floral displays are typical.

Święto Wniebowzięcia (Feast of the Assumption). On 15th August, thousands make the pilgrimage to the monastery of Jasna Góra in Częstochowa to see the icon of the Black Madonna and to pray for forgiveness and healing. The icon was apparently painted on an old tabletop salvaged from the Nazareth residence of the Holy Family.

An old reputation for tolerance

The Jewish faith used to refer to Poland as 'Polin', *po* meaning 'here' and *lin* meaning 'rest' in Hebrew. Jews who fled persecution in Germany and Bohemia in large numbers between the 12th and 15th centuries chose Poland as one of the few countries in which they felt safe (see section 1.2.1 for more). Similarly, in the 15th and 16th centuries Protestant Scots fleeing the Counter Reformation and Huguenots escaping the Inquisition sought refuge in Poland, such was its reputation for tolerance.

Black Madonna of Częstochowa

Where's Dolittle when you need him?

Animals in Poland are apparently blessed with the power of speech at midnight on Wigilia. Alas, there's never anyone around to hear them – everyone is in church taking Mass.

Dzień Wszystkich Świętych (All Saints' Day). The most solemn of national holidays, held on 1st November, is devoted to the dead. Many Poles spend the day graveside, visiting old family members. At dusk, chrysanthemums and candles or votives are used to decorate the graves. On the following day, All Souls' Day, prayers are offered for the souls of the departed, helping them on their way to heaven (or not).

Wigilia (Christmas Eve). Wigilia translates as 'waiting', and on 24th December Polish families gather to anticipate the birth of Christ with a large traditional meal, before which there is an exchange of good wishes and the breaking and sharing of *opłatek*, the Christmas wafer. Hay is placed under the tablecloth (as per the Bethlehem stable), stalks of which can be removed and apparently used to predict the future.

Boże Narodzenie (Christmas Day). Christmas Day begins with *pasterka*, the Midnight Mass, after which a more subdued day (than Wigilia) unfolds, featuring animal-shaped bread, carols and family gatherings. In theory, all forms of work – cooking, wood chopping, etc. – are put on hold.

Święto Trzech Króli (Epiphany). Poland celebrates the arrival of the three kings on January 6th with a national holiday (as reinstated in 2012). Processions (live animals included) are held and blessed chalk is used to inscribe C, B and M above doorways (as per the three magi, Casper, Balthazar and Melchior).

Karol Józef Wojtyła

(1920 – 2005)

The Polish pope Karol Wojtyła was born near Kraków in 1920. His studies in philosophy and drama at Jagiellonian University were interrupted by the war – the Nazis made him work in a quarry – after which he switched to theology. By 1964 he was Archbishop of Kraków and three years later became the youngest cardinal ever appointed by Rome. Under Soviet rule, Wojtyła stood up to the regime, performing outdoor masses attended by thousands, until the government relented and allowed the construction of Arka Pana, the Lord's Ark Church in Nowa Huta, Kraków. As the first Slavic Pope (he was ennobled in 1978), he returned to Poland, met with Lech Wałęsa, and offered courage and inspiration with his message, *nie lękajcie się* (have no fear). When communism fell apart, many, Mikhail Gorbachev included, acknowledged the Pope's pivotal role. Whilst his conservatism on issues such as homosexuality and birth control caused controversy, in Poland Pope John Paul II's popularity never waned. The country went into national mourning when he died on 2nd April 2005. Six years later he was beatified.

Two houses, one president

Democracy, as enshrined in 1997 in the Constitution of the Republic of Poland, is a relatively new phenomenon for the modern Pole. Even though elections were held during the years of Communist rule, with most prominent critics of the regime in jail or dead the choice of candidates was limited, and anyway, the results were predetermined (i.e. fixed). Today, Poland operates a multi-party political system with a democratically elected president sitting at the head of a bicameral parliament consisting of lower house, the Sejm, and upper house, the Senat. Local governmental bodies are also elected, covering provincial, county and municipal jurisdictions, as are ministers for the European Parliament.

The president of Poland is the head of state and the supreme commander of the armed forces. Elections for the post are held every five years and the incumbent can serve a maximum of two terms. Parliamentary elections take place every four years (suffrage begins aged 18). The 460 members of the Sejm are elected by proportional representation, the 100-strong Senat, by contrast, is returned using a first-past-the-post system. Executive power lies with the prime minister, appointed by the president from the party (or parties in coalition) holding a majority in the Sejm, and with the council of ministers, which is also appointed by the president but chosen by the prime minister and approved by the Sejm by way of a vote of confidence.

The Poles at the polls

Given the upheavals of their recent past, it is not surprising to learn that most Poles are politically aware and ready for a healthy argument on the issues of the day – unemployment, crime, immigration and the Church are often on the menu. However, this interest in current affairs isn't reflected in voter turnout figures. Only around half of those registered to vote actually make it to a polling station. The near constant whiff of corruption (whether real or imagined) has left many disillusioned with the political process. Others are kept away by apathy. One issue that does elicit common interest, however, is Europe. More than 75 per cent of Poles said *tak* (yes) to EU accession in the referendum of 2003 (turnout ran to 58.85 per cent), and the benefits of membership – billions of Euros have been ploughed into the country's economy and infrastructure – are hard to ignore.

Three memorable statesmen

Józef Piłsudski. The major political figure of the interwar years assumed supreme command of the armed forces in 1918 and became provisional chief-of-state of the newly independent Poland. He retired from politics in 1923 but returned to the fray three years later, in the bloody May Coup d'État that overthrew Wincenty Witos' government amid economic crises and widespread civil unrest. Piłsudski went on to become de facto dictator of Poland until his death in 1935.

Józef Pilsudski

(1867 – 1935)

"To be defeated and not submit, is victory; to be victorious and rest on one's laurels, is defeat."

General Władysław Sikorski. A hero of both the First World War and the war against the Soviets in the early 1920s, Sikorski served as commander-in-chief and prime minister in the early years of the Second Republic but fell from favour after Piłsudski staged his coup. He rose to prominence again in the Second World War, leading the Polish government in exile and again taking charge of the Polish Army. Sikorski's insistence that the Red Cross investigate the Katyn massacre of 1940 gave Stalin the chance to break of ties with Poland. He died in a plane crash in Gibraltar in 1943.

Lech Wałęsa. The shipyard electrician turned trade union activist who, as leader of the Solidarność movement did most to secure the momentous Round Table Agreement of 4th April 1989. It led to the semi-free parliamentary elections of June that year, initiating the fall of communism in Poland and beyond (see section 1.2.3 for more). Wałęsa was awarded the Nobel Peace Prize in 1983 and served as President of Poland from 1990 to 1995.

The main political parties

On the right

Platforma Obywatelska (PO) (Civic Platform). A liberal conservative (centre-right) party founded in 2001 in opposition to abortion, same-sex marriage and drug decriminalisation but in favour of environmental sustainability and social justice issues. The Polish president elected in 2010, Bronisław Komorowski, is in the PO, and the party was retuned as the largest single party in both the Sejm and the Senat in the general election a year later (they formed a coalition with a junior partner, the Polish People's Party, and supplied PM, Donald Tusk).

224

1. Identity: the foundations of Polish culture   2. Literature and philosophy   3. Art, architecture and design   4. Music, theatre, and comedy   5. Cinema and fashion   6. Media and communications   7. Food and drink   **8. Living culture: the state of modern Poland**

Prawo i Sprawiedliwość (PiS) (Law and Justice). The second largest party at the 2011 elections (having been in power six years earlier) was founded in 2001 by twin brothers Lech and Jaroslaw Kaczyński. The PiS supports anti-corruption measures and takes a sceptic's stance on Europe. Some policies have drawn accusations of homophobia.

On the left

Ruch Palikota (RP) (Palikot's Movement). A recent arrival on the political scene, founded by Janusz Palikot in 2011, the RP is a liberal left party that takes an openly anti-Church stance and supports same-sex marriage, abortion on demand and the legalisation of cannabis. The party is popular with younger voters and counts Poland's first openly gay and first transgender MPs amongst its representatives in the Sejm.

Sojusz Lewicy Demokratycznej (SLD) (Democratic Left Alliance). A social democratic party with Communist roots formed in 1991. Since sweeping to victory in the 2001 election with party leader Leszek Miller serving as prime minister, the SLD has experienced a huge downturn in popularity, thanks largely to corruption scandals. Much of its remaining support migrated to the as yet untainted Palikot's Movement in the 2011 election.

In the centre

Polskie Stronnictwo Ludowe (PSL) (The Polish People's Party). A centrist party formed in 1990, with a pronounced agrarian platform advocating state intervention in agriculture and the slowing down of privatisation, whilst opposing same-sex marriage, abortion, euthanasia and the decriminalisation of drugs. The PSL's leader is ex-prime minister Waldemar Pawlak. The party has been involved in four coalition governments, in 1993, 2001, 2007 and 2011 (despite only gaining 28 seats in the Sejm and two in the Senat in 2011).

On the world stage

Poland has the 21st largest economy in the world, with a GDP of $721.3 billion (purchasing power parity).

Job descriptions

The labour force in Poland numbers 17.6 million people, divided thus:

Agriculture – 14.8 per cent

Industry – 30.7 per cent

Service industries – 54.5 per cent

The national bank

Poland's central bank is the Narodowy Bank Polski (NBP), which is responsible for issuing currency, setting interest rates and acting as a regulatory body for other banks in the country. The NBP was founded in 1945 and was one of only two banks permitted to operate under the Communist regime; the other being PKO Bank Polski, which dealt with personal accounts and which is still going strong today.

The comeback kid

Poland is one of the great success stories of modern economics. At the end of the Communist era, the country faced food shortages, perilous international debt and soaring inflation (for a while it reached 500 per cent), yet two decades on, Poland has the sixth largest economy in Europe. The turnaround has been achieved through industrious entrepreneurship; by the hard graft of a skilled workforce, political will and no small amount of European funding (Poland has been the largest net recipient of EU cash, allotted €67 billion in the 2007-13 budget). Poland duly has the distinction of being the sole EU member to avoid recession in the 2008/9 downturn.

Naturally gifted: sources of wealth

Poland has traditionally relied on its minerals for wealth, and the production of coal, copper, sulphur, iron and steel remain key to the new market economy, with the industrial sector generating a third of GDP. A strong manufacturing base, featuring everything from ships and cars to electronics and pharmaceuticals, has helped bolster this area of the economy. By contrast, Polish agriculture suffers with poor productivity; even though the country is a significant producer of potatoes, rye, sugar beets, rapeseed and cattle, and one in seven Poles work in agriculture, the sector only contributes 3.4 per cent of GDP. The remaining, lion's share of Polish income is derived from the service industries, where tourism, IT, retail and banking have been responsible for much of the country's recent growth.

The old National Bank of Poland

The Stock Exchange

Things could be worse (a lot worse)

Despite the economic growth of recent years, the lot of the average Pole still has room for improvement. Unemployment hovers stubbornly around the ten per cent mark, whilst GDP per capita of $18,800 places Poland 64th in the global league table. And yet, it seems, most Poles prefer the market economy to the state-controlled model pursued in the Communist era. In relative terms, the individual is more prosperous than once they were, and the attendant surveys regularly reveal four out of five Poles to be 'very' or 'quite' happy with their lives. Indeed, the Poles' refusal to stop spending may have been a contributory factor in the country's success at dodging recession in 2009.

The safety net

The welfare system in Poland is managed by the Zakład Ubezpieczeń Społecznych, (ZUS) (Social Insurance Department), which operates under the auspices of the Ministry of Labour and Social Policy. Workers and employers make mandatory contributions to pensions (the state variant can be taken by women at 60 and by men at 65), sickness pay and maternity benefit. A separate labour fund, the Fundusz Pracy, handles unemployment benefit. In common with most Western countries, Poland is concerned about the increasing burden its aging population will place on the welfare state: at present Poland has 26 pensioners for every 100 people of working age; the projection for 2035 is 46 pensioners for every 100 workers. The government is implementing complex reforms in an effort to manage this aging population.

The stock exchange

The Polish stock exchange has had three incarnations. The first, the Warsaw Mercantile Exchange (Giełda Kupiecka w Warszawie), was in operation in the 19th century; then came the Warsaw Money Exchange (Giełda Pieniężna w Warszawie) during the interwar years of the 20th century; to be followed by the present edifice, the Warsaw Stock Exchange (WSE) (Giełda Papierów Wartościowych w Warszawie), in 1991. The WSE opened with only five companies, but has grown rapidly into one of Europe's largest exchanges with over 400 companies listed on its main market. The exchange has lived in the ultra-modern Exchange Centre since 2000, having moved from the former headquarters of the Polish Communist Party.

1. Identity: the foundations of Polish culture

2. Literature and philosophy

3. Art, architecture and design

4. Music, theatre, and comedy

5. Cinema and fashion

6. Media and communications

7. Food and drink

8. Living culture: the state of modern Poland

8.5 Keeping order: the courts, crime and the police

The Polish code

Poland has a civil system of law. It takes the Kodeks cywilny (the Polish civil code), a vast collection of codified statutes, as its primary legal source. The code was formalised in 1964, completed after years of disarray in the legal system, although has been subsequently amended on several occasions to keep pace with Poland's newly democratised make-up and, in particular, its accession into the EU. As with most continental civil law systems, the proceedings in Polish courts are inquisitorial rather than adversarial in nature and are presided over by a judge, appointed for life by the president. The judges aren't called upon to make interpretations of the law; they follow the code. The legal system has struggled to keep up with the dramatic speed of change in modern Poland and, perhaps inevitably, has a reputation (its courts at least) for being over-laden and slow.

The court system

Common courts. Adjudicating in criminal, civil, family and labour cases, the common courts consist of 315 district courts, 45 regional courts (which deal with serious crimes and hear appeals from the district courts) and 11 appeal courts (hearing appeals from the regional courts).

Military courts. Provincial and garrison courts dealing with crimes committed by soldiers and military employees.

Administrative courts. Comprising 14 regional courts with judicial control over matters concerning public administrative bodies.

The Supreme Court. Warsaw's Supreme Court, or Sąd Najwyższy, hears appeals against judgements made in the lower courts and passes resolutions to clarify specific legal issues.

Supreme Court

Crime scene

The Poles are as law abiding as most Europeans. The murder rate, for example, is slightly lower than in France, slightly higher than in the UK. Car theft is a problem, both internally and cross-border, giving rise to the old joke 'Come to Poland – your car's already here', and pickpocketing is relatively common in city centres. Organised crime has grown in recent years, fuelled by the production of designer drugs and the manufacture of counterfeit cigarettes and alcohol. Encouragingly, though, the overall crime rate in Poland appears to fall year on year.

Keeping the peace: the Polish police

For a long time the Polish police had form; a hard-to-shake reputation for arbitrary repression that stretched back to the Communist era, when the Milicja obywatelska, the Citizens' Militia as they were inaptly known, were widely despised, particularly for the way they dealt with the street protests of the 1970s and '80s. However, the image of the Policja, as they were renamed, has improved significantly since 1989. A recent national survey (carried out by the police themselves, it must be said), showed an approval rate of 72 per cent for the forces of law and order. There are, of course, dissenting voices, often amongst younger Poles, as the appearance of the offensive graffito, 'HWDP', testifies (it's an acronym for a vulgar phrase urging a particular type of sexual assault).

Ripping yarns: two Polish serial killers

Lucjan Staniak.
Staniak began raping and disembowelling young blonde women in 1964, announcing the murders to the press in poetic letters written in spidery red ink. 'There is no happiness without tears, no life without death. Beware! I am going to make you cry', read the first missive. He became known as the 'Red Spider' (*Czerwony pająk*). Once caught, Staniak confessed to over 20 murders and was sent to an asylum for the insane in Katowice in 1967.

Władysław Mazurkiewicz.
Dubbed the 'Gentleman Murderer' (*Morderca dżentelmen*) on account of his elegant dress and manner, Mazurkiewicz enjoyed an expensive lifestyle maintained by the proceeds from a series of violent robberies carried out in Warsaw and Kraków in the 1950s. Most of the robberies ended in the victim's murder. When the police finally caught Mazurkiewicz, he readily confessed to at least 30 counts of murder and was hanged in Montelupich Prison, Kraków, in 1957.

Last man hanging

Capital punishment was abolished in Poland on 1st April 1998. The last person executed was actually hung ten years earlier; Stanisław Czabański, put to death at Montelupich Prison in Kraków for the rape and murder of a woman in Tarnów.

The Butcher of Mokotów Prison

In the early, post-war days of Stalinist rule, opponents of the state were often executed by means of a bullet to the base of the skull. The prime venue for such executions was Mokotów Prison in Warsaw; and the prime exponent, staff sergeant Piotr Śmietański, known as the Butcher of Mokotów Prison. Śmietański was personally responsible for the deaths of hundreds of anti-Communist activists. At some point in the 1960s, like many of his victims, he simply disappeared without trace.

Police divisions

The national police force employs 103,000 officers and 12,000 civilian staff, most of them arranged amongst 16 provincial forces. Each force typically comprises:

Policja prewencyjna (Preventative police). General law enforcement officers including patrol, traffic, anti-terrorist and riot police.

Policja kryminalna (Criminal police). Investigating serious and violent crime.

Straż miejska (Municipal officers). Employed by the local authorities, and given only limited powers.

Behind bars: the prison system

Polish prisons suffer with an image problem. For decades they were places of torture and execution, and in subsequent years, in the later 20th century, a lack of investment engendered poor conditions and overcrowding. The current prison infrastructure, featuring 87 prisons and 70 pre-trial facilities, and housing more than 80,000 prisoners (about three per cent of whom are women), is troubled by its age. The penal institution in Nowy Wiśnicz, for example, is a former monastery which, having been built in 1635, makes Wronki, the largest prison in the country with 1,400 inmates, seem relatively youthful at the tender age of 120. A programme of modernisation is underway.

Most improved student

Sweeping reforms have dramatically improved public education in Poland in recent years. At the end of the 1990s, a system largely unchanged since the Communist era was replaced under a series of new education acts. Everything was reviewed, from administration and finance to teachers' rights, whilst schools were encouraged to build their own curricula within a pre-determined framework. The results have been remarkable. The proportion of children leaving school early dropped well below the EU average; and the numbers completing upper secondary education rose well above (schooling here is now compulsory up to the age of 18). Language teaching, in particular, has benefited from the reforms. Poland now ranks amongst the top 15 OECD countries for the overall quality of its education provision.

Going private

Private (non-state) education – from primary schools to universities – has been available in Poland since 1989. The number of such institutions – many of which are run by religious organisations – is rising rapidly, even whilst the expense of private schooling puts it beyond the reach of most, and also whilst the standard of state schooling exceeds that provided in much of the private sector.

How the schooling system breaks down

Pre-school education. The first level of the education system is compulsory for all six-year-old children. Primary reading skills and basic mathematics are taught.

Elementary school (duration six years). Children aged seven to thirteen learn about Polish language and literature, history, biology, geography, physics, PE, the arts, environment and technology. In grades one to three all subjects are taught by one teacher; in grades four to six each subject has a specialist tutor.

Teaching notes

At 99 per cent, the literacy rate in Poland is amongst the highest in the world.

Poland spends around 30,000 euros educating each of its students (the USA spends approximately double that figure).

Three out of ten Poles aged 25 to 34 have a university education.

Performance related pay

Prior to 2007, teachers were paid according to the length of time in the profession. Under new guidelines, salaries are calculated on tasks performed and results achieved, as well as professional experience.

Top of the class

Although Poland has no Ivy League or Oxbridge as such, two particular universities have an outstanding pedigree and reputation:

University of Warsaw (Uniwersytet Warszawski). Founded in 1816, the University of Warsaw is the most prestigious in the country. Enrolment is 53,700.

Jagiellonian University in Krakow (Uniwersytet Jagielonski). The oldest university in Poland (established in 1364) and second oldest in Europe boasts Copernicus and Pope John Paul II amongst its alumni. Enrolment is 46,545.

The prom

Three months before taking the *matura*, students get glammed up for the Polish equivalent of a high school senior prom.

Gymnasium (duration three years). Students between the ages of 13 and 16 study Polish, foreign languages (English is the most popular, followed by German) history, mathematic, physics, PE, chemistry, geography, biology and environmental studies. The focus is on a wide variety of subjects taught at a basic level, thereby guiding the student towards an informed choice on which stream of secondary education to enter.

Secondary school (duration three to five years). After Gymnasium, students can enrol in General Secondary, Specialised or Technical Schools. Those who stay the course will take the *egzamin dojrzałości* (also known as the *matura*), a standardised national secondary school exam. A fourth option, the Basic Vocational School, allows students to graduate with a diploma. Students hoping to progress to university after secondary school must also gain a *świadectwo dojrzałości* certificate.

Jagiellonian University

232

Higher education. After secondary school, students can pursue higher education in universities, polytechnics and academies specialising in everything from medicine to agriculture. Warsaw is the biggest academic centre with the largest student enrolment and the greatest number of higher education institutions.

Degrees of separation: higher education
Higher education has grown significantly over the last decade. The number of dedicated institutions has increased five-fold while the quantity of students has quadrupled (Poland now has around two million). Tuition in the state-run system (there are 138 government-funded centres of higher learning) is free but the competition to get in is tough, with as many as ten candidates fighting for each place (depending on subject). Poland also has an extensive network of private universities, some 300 in all (serving the biggest private sector tertiary intake in Europe), most of which focus on vocational training. State-backed loans can be applied for to help with tuition fees. Private institutions don't receive any direct government funding, although they are lobbying hard for the introduction of fees into the public sector in the hope that it will level out the playing field. However, many Poles remain convinced that students shouldn't be able to 'buy an education'. Equally, a lot of academics, as well as members of the public, are sceptical about the quality of learning at many private universities.

Carnival: the big blow out

The parties and balls of Carnival take the edge off the Polish winter between New Year's Day and Lent. In the countryside, particularly in the mountains, the celebrations include a bonfire and a *kulig* (sleigh ride). Mulled wine, beer and *bigos* keep the blood flowing. On the last Thursday before Lent (Fat Thursday), the country gorges on *pączki* (see section 7.1.3), and then the three days running up to Ash Wednesday mark the climax of Carnival: everyone dresses up, dances, drinks, eats and turns the music up loud – doing all the things that are off limits during Lent.

Don't forget about

Mother's Day (26th May).

Granny's Day (21st January).

Children's Day (1st June).

Taking a day off

The Poles work long hours but are rewarded with a generous holiday entitlement – 20 days a year up to ten years' service and 26 days thereafter. Throw in 13 bank holidays and the picture is rosier still (although the Poles aren't awarded days off in lieu for bank holidays that fall on weekends). Since the fall of communism, the Poles have increasingly filled their spare time with the same things as the rest of the Western world: taking holidays; visiting restaurants, shopping malls, theatres and pubs; watching TV or surfing the internet; attempting DIY or tending to the garden or allotment. They also love the great outdoors; taking to the lakes, beaches and mountains at every available opportunity for fishing, water sports, hiking, camping and skiing. Above everything else, however, the Poles are innately social, and duly spend as much of their downtime as possible visiting friends and relatives.

The public holidays

Nowy Rok New Year's Day (1st January).

Objawienie Pańskie Epiphany (6th January).

Wielka Niedziela Easter Sunday (moveable).

Lany Poniedziałek Easter Monday (moveable).

Święto Państwowe May Day (1st May).

Święto Narodowe Trzeciego Maja Constitution Day (3rd May).

Pierwszy dzień Zielonych Świątek Pentecost Sunday (seventh Sunday after Easter).

Dzień Bożego Ciała Corpus Christi (ninth Thursday after Easter).

Wniebowzięcie Najświętszej Maryi Panny Assumption (15th August) (also Polish Army Day).

Wszystkich Świętych All Saints' Day (1st November).

Narodowe Święto Niepodległości Independence Day (11th November).

Pierwszy dzień Bożego Narodzenia Christmas Day (25th December – 'First Day of Christmas').

Drugi dzień Bożego Narodzenia Boxing Day (26th December – 'Second Day of Christmas').

No place like home

Holidays are important in Poland – most people devote around ten per cent of their income to vacationing – although they take fewer than their Western neighbours. Typically, they take one extended break a year (usually for a fortnight), and interject the rest of the year with several long weekends. The Poles are also far more likely to holiday on home turf than to venture abroad.

The cooling breezes and sandy beaches of the Baltic coastline have been a big summer draw for centuries. Sopot is the grandest of the grand old resorts – a place where Fidel Castro, Marlene Dietrich and Omar Sharif used to holiday. Today, it maintains its reputation for exclusivity and still attracts the well-heeled and the famous. The Mazurian Lakes (one of various Polish lake districts) and the Carpathian mountains are similarly popular, and kinder on the wallet. Holidaymakers also head for Poland's historic spas – part of a tradition dating back to the 13th century – where the emphasis on health and well-being is perhaps stronger than at spa resorts in other parts of the world. In winter, resorts like Zakopane have traditionally been popular with Polish skiers, although more now make for cheaper alternatives in Italy and Slovakia. When they do venture abroad, the Poles favour extended weekend breaks in Barcelona, Paris, London and Rome (which was inundated with Poles in 2010 visiting for the beatification of Pope John Paul II).

Two unusual festivals

On the **first day of spring** (the vernal equinox) across Poland, an effigy of Marzanna, the scarecrow-like symbol of winter, is drowned or burned.

On **4th December**, Katowice celebrates Barbara, patron saint of miners. The miners wear elaborate costumes and the locals pray for their safety.

Three days in May

The holiday period that runs from 1st to 3rd May is known as *majówka*, 'The Picnic'. Most banks, businesses, government offices and shops close. The first day of the three, Labour Day, is the state holiday that in Soviet days featured government-led celebrations and parades in front of the party elite. Today it is a less politicised affair. The following day is known as Flag Day, introduced in 2004 to commemorate the day the Polish army planted their flag on the Victory Column during the Battle of Berlin in 1945. Finally, 3rd May is Constitution Day, marking the signing of Poland's constitution in 1791 (see section 1.2.2 for more).

A sporting gesture

At the 1980 Moscow Olympics, Polish pole vault jumper Władysław Kozakiewicz famously celebrated winning the gold medal by making an obscene gesture to the hostile Russian crowd, who had been supporting their own man, Konstantin Volkov. The gesture, often called the *bras d'honneur* (arm of honour), signified to many the Poles' resentment of Russian influence over Eastern Europe, if not towards communism itself. Kozakiewicz defected to the West in 1984; nevertheless in Poland his iconic gesture is still known as the *gest Kozakiewicza*.

How to do the *gest Kozakiewicza*:

1. Stretch out your right arm, upturned with fist clenched.

2. Slap the palm of your left hand on the midway point of the outstretched arm.

3. At the same time, raise your right forearm and with clenched fist 90 degrees into an upright position in an aggressive manner.

4. It helps if you also wear tight red shorts and grin like a maniac (as Kozakiewicz did).

Cheering from the sidelines

The Poles love their sport. For years, it was closely controlled and used, like much else, for propaganda, but today the nation enjoys its games unfettered by government intervention. However, it must also be said that most Poles today enjoy their sport from a seated position, perhaps in the company of a beer or two. Spectating is a lot more popular that participation – only a third of Poles play a sport more than once a month; most don't play at all.

The beautiful game

Football is far and away the most popular sport in Poland. Millions participate actively and passively all year round. In the main they're watching the Ekstraklasa, the premier division of the Polish professional league formed in 1927. The Ekstraklasa comprises 16 teams, with Wisła Kraków and Legia Warsaw notable amongst the big names and drawing more fans than the average premier league gate of around 8,400.

The Polish national team, nicknamed the Białe Orły (the White Eagles), enjoys passionate support, even whilst performances in recent times have fallen well short of those produced by the 'golden' side of the 1970s and early '80s. The Poles fondly recall players like Grzegorz Lato and Kazimierz Deyna, and manger Kazimierz Górski, who won Olympic gold and silver in 1972 and 1976 respectively, and came third at the World Cups in West Germany in 1974 and Spain in 1982 (that time under a different coach, Antoni Piechniczek). In more recent years, football in Poland has been in the news for the wrong reasons with several major instances of hooliganism and ongoing investigations into widespread corruption that have seen eight clubs docked points or relegated as punishment.

The also rans: Poland's other sports

Speedway – men on motorbikes hurtling around an oval dirt track without any brakes – has been popular in Poland since the 1930s. The current premier division, the Ekstraliga żużlowa, comprises eight teams and draws the highest average attendance of any sport in the country, with around 8,500 spectators per race meeting. Notable riders include Jerzy Szczakiel and Tomasz Gollob, the only Poles to win the Individual Speedway World Championship, in 1973 and 2010. The national speedway team is also a major force, being ten-time world champions, including a three-year run at the top from 2009 to 2011.

Formula One has won an appreciative Polish audience in recent years, thanks largely to the exploits of Robert Kubica, the first Polish racing driver to compete at the top level. Kubica won his first race in 2008 in the Canadian Grand Prix. Volleyball also has legion fans, with both the men's and women's national sides riding high in the world rankings. Handball is similarly popular, whilst basketball, ice hockey, boxing and athletics also draw players and spectators. Finally, there's ringo – a sport

Clowning glory

On a famous night in October 1973, the Polish national football team drew 1-1 with England at Wembley Stadium and secured qualification to the 1974 World Cup, eliminating their opponents from the competition in the process. The hero of the evening was Jan Tomaszewski, the Polish goalkeeper, who, despite having been labelled 'a clown' by some in the media prior to the fixture, produced the man of the match performance that denied England the victory they required. Tomaszewski went on to become a prominent football pundit, well known for his controversial views, before turning to politics – in 2011 he was elected to the Sejm representing Łódź for the Law and Justice party.

invented by Polish fencer Włodzimierz Strzyżewski in 1959. Ringo involves throwing a rubber ring, 3cm thick and 17cm wide, back and forth over a volleyball net.

Four sporting legends

Irena Kirszenstein-Szewińska. A revered sprinter and one of the greatest female athletes in track and field history, Kirszenstein-Szewińska won medals in four consecutive Olympic Games between 1964 and 1976, including three golds. She was also the first woman to concurrently hold world records at 100m, 200m and 400m distances.

Adam Małysz. Recently retired, Małysz was one of the greatest ski jumpers of all time and probably the biggest sports star in Poland in the modern era. Millions would tune in to watch his performances on TV – a phenomenon that became known as Małyszomania. Małysz' honours include four World Championship and four World Cup titles (including three in a row in 2001, 2002 and 2003).

Grzegorz Lato. Capped 100 times for his country, scoring 45 goals along the way, Lato is probably Poland's most famous football hero. He's best remembered for his performances in the 1974 World Cup, where seven goals earned him the prestigious Golden Boot (awarded to the tournament's top scorer) and helped his country secure third place. In 2008, Lato was elected president of the PZPN, the Polish Football Association.

Wanda Rutkiewicz. An inspirational, charismatic mountaineer, Rutkiewicz conquered Mount Everest in 1978, becoming only the third woman to reach the summit. Eight years later, she was the first woman to stand on top of K2. Rutkiewicz died in 1992 in the final stages of an attempted ascent of Kanchenjunga, another Himalayan giant, the third highest mountain on Earth (it would have been her ninth peak over 8,000 metres).

Adam Malysz of Poland takes 2nd place during the FIS Ski Jumping World Cup Vierschanzentournee (Four Hills Tournament) in January 2011 in Innsbruck, Austria.